Recreation Rooms

BY A. J. HARMON, A.I.A.

GROSSET
GOOD LIFE
BOOKS

PUBLISHERS • GROSSET & DUNLAP • NEW YORK

A FILMWAYS COMPANY

Text and illustrations by A. J. Harmon
Cover photograph by Mort Engel

1938684

Contents

1
Recreation Rooms

Fifty years ago a recreation room in the average home would have been almost unthinkable. The parlor was used only on Sunday, for tea when the minister came to call, or for funerals. The dining room was the family room. The whole family worked, children went to bed at seven o'clock, and if the man of the house had any time left after a day at the shop or factory, he probably preferred to have a beer in the peace and quiet of the kitchen.

True, in the days before income taxes, the very wealthy included a billiard room (for men only) for quiet relaxation with cigars and brandy after dinner. Sometimes a ballroom, such as the East Room of the White House, would be included for sumptuous galas. However, even these rooms were often used for other things. Mrs. Adams found the East Room to be a convenient place for drying the laundry.

Now, with increased leisure time and the five-day workweek (even the four-day workweek in some areas), the recreation room is experiencing unequaled popularity. It cannot be called a rebirth because we did not really have such rooms before. Of course, in the late 1950s and early 1960s, before the government latched onto bomb shelters to bolster the sagging construction business, there was a flurry of magazine articles that flushed a number of slick salesmen onto the streets selling recreation room remodeling packages for the basement. There are still companies that specialize in doing over basements, but they usually manage to sell you on what they can do, not what you want done or what is best for your house. These "specialists" should be avoided.

Your Kind of Recreation Room

A recreation room means different things to different people. Webster's describes "recreation" as, among other things, "refreshment of strength and spirits after toil." In this sense every room in the house should qualify as a recreation room, but Webster's also defines recreate as "to create anew, especially from the imagination." Every family should have a room all members can go to let their imaginations soar and their spirits ramble. A room where, like a vast library, every shelf contains illusion, knowledge, and escape. A

A recreation room for children, barnlike in effect, with indestructible and easy-to-clean surfaces.

room where shoes on the coffee table or a spilled soft drink is not a disaster.

It is simply not feasible that, as some books and magazine articles would have it, the efforts of one rainy weekend can transform a dark, damp basement into a thing of beauty and a joy forever. And if you believe that putting a Ping-Pong table in the garage or attic is going to lure the children out of the living room so you can have cocktails in peace and quiet, you are sadly mistaken. Halfway measures will not work. It takes thinking, time, and money.

Any new room or living space is going to change the way you live in your house, and it should be regarded as an investment, improving the livability and value of your property. A recreation room should not be a place where you banish furniture you don't want in the living room. This kind of recreation room too often becomes simply a second-class living room. If you allow this to happen, no one in the family will want to use the room, and guests taken there for cocktails or bridge will get the feeling that you don't trust them in the room with the good furniture.

Most depressing of all is the typical basement recreation room with high basement windows, low ceilings, and dangerously steep stairs. This is the kind often glamorized in magazines and advertisements selling paneling or acoustical tile. The basement, which at first thought may seem to be the most logical location, is usually the poorest place to invest in a recreation room. It is generally difficult to get to, so it will be underused, but more important, it is difficult to get out of in case of fire.

If a basement does not have a second exit, and one that gives quick and easy access to the exterior cannot be provided, do not consider it as a possible location for a recreation room.

For adults, a recreation room with fire pit, built-in sofas, bar, and billiard table.

How Will the Room Be Used?

The next thing to consider is how the room is to be used. If it will be a place to enjoy creative hobbies such as sewing, photography, or painting, or games such as chess and serious bridge, it can be located in a quiet area of the house. However, if it is to be used for woodworking or trumpet practice, it should be away from the bedrooms and wherever else members of the family might object to the noise.

If a recreation room is to be used often for large parties, birthday celebrations, and such, it should be either near the kitchen or have its own facilities for serving food. You might also want to design it with its own entrance so that guests do not have to go through the house to get to it. Such a recreation room may require separate closets for coats and storage and a handy second bathroom.

When Will the Room Be Used?

The design and location of a recreation room will depend not only on how the room is to be used, but when. Is it to be just a room for the children to play in when it is raining, or is it to be used every day after school for homework? Will it be used mostly in the winter when it is too cold to relax on the porch or in the garden? If so, you might want to include a fireplace or supply additional heat ducts from the furnace. If it is to be used all year round, you might want to include air conditioning.

If it is going to be used during the day, natural light should be provided. Sunlight might not seem important to you if you plan to use the room mostly at night, but psychologically the possibility of having natural light and ventilation is essential to dispel the impression of dank air and mustiness.

Who Will Use the Room?

Who will use the recreation room is as important as how and when it will be used. If it is to be used for children's hard and rough play, careful attention will have to be paid to the selection of materials and the placement of windows and a fireplace. You will want to use materials that do not soil easily and can be cleaned quickly when they do, but are soft enough not to scrape knees and elbows.

If the recreation room is to be used for an elaborate electric train layout or a work area for making model ships or planes, you may want a separate room or space to give other family members equal time for Ping-Pong or pool. It is a mistake, however, to construct elaborate built-ins for young children. They outgrow them too quickly and many are just as happy with some boxes and pieces of plywood they can use to put together fanciful designs that will change day to day from fort to schoolhouse to hospital.

Where to Locate the Room

Who will use the room will also play an important part in selecting the right location for a recreation room.

If adults and their guests will be using the room at night, and children and their friends during the day, locate the recreation room in a part of the house where you can build a separate entrance off the driveway. Children do not mind traipsing through a kitchen or another room to get to the recreation room, but grown-up guests might. Too, children seldom stay in one spot very long. The added exit will cut down on some of the traffic to and from the room to pick up toys for play, put away bikes left out in the rain, meet the ice cream man, and go next door to Billy's or Sally's. All this trooping through the kitchen can play havoc with the cook's nerves.

Children do not enjoy being shunted off by themselves. They can effortlessly find hundreds of excuses and questions to put to adults, especially if it means interrupting a bridge game or serious discussion. Any recreation room will have to be pretty special to keep them in it when the adults are concentrated in the living room and do not want to be bothered. And since children do need some supervision, it can be a mistake to isolate them in the basement or in an out-of-the-way room.

When designing a room that is to be used by both children and adults, design it basically for the adults. Children can adapt much better to an adult recreation room than adults can to a children's recreation room.

If the room is to be used only by members of the family, place it where it can be reached from the main rooms of the house. In fact, if space is not available within the house itself, the recreation room can be in a separate structure. A separate structure with a loggia connecting it to the house is often the best recreation room and can cost no more than one in the basement. A separate pavilion will add considerably more to the value of your property than almost any recreation room in the basement, regardless of how well finished the latter is. A pavilion will also keep the noise away from the house, along with the traffic and other distractions that can occur when a recreation room is part of the house proper.

2
Professional Help and Legal Regulations

Whether you are converting existing space or building an addition for a recreation room, the most important consideration is design. You may be capable of doing the carpentry and necessary electrical work, but if the effort is not centered around a good design, all your labor will have been wasted. Simply because you can drive a car does not mean you can design one. The same is true of a home: putting a pool table in some unused space is not the same as adding a recreation room. The elements to be considered are materials, heating, lighting, ventilation, access, and how all of these can increase the value of your property.

You may feel able to handle all the work yourself, both the design and the actual construction, but most people find as the work progresses that they need and should have had professional help. This is not to say that if you want to enclose the garage and make it into a recreation room, you must hire an architect, contractor, and interior decorator, but neither should you avoid professional help and advice. Many times a simple, and seemingly offhand, suggestion by an architect can save you time and money and improve your house. For instance, you may be planning to convert your garage into a recreation room, not realizing that the room will be flooded from the spring rains. Or you might be all ready to build a recreation room and pool, until the architect points out that the zoning regulations in your area do not permit it.

The Architect

You may not think you need the services of an architect to design and supervise the construction of a recreation room, and you may be right, but the best way to find out is to let the architect tell you. The amount of money you have to spend is no indication one way or the other. In fact, the lower your budget, the more important it is to spend the money wisely, getting all you can for it. An architect will not necessarily save you money, but he will see that you get the most for what you have to spend, and that the recreation room is right for you and your house. He will plan, design, find the best contractors, and supervise the work for you. Or, if you intend to do the work yourself, he will provide the design and expert advice on the best way to do things with the least expensive materials.

Working with an Architect

Finding an architect is not difficult, but finding one who is willing to take on a small job such as a recreation room may take time. Call or write the local chapter of the American Institute of Architects (A.I.A.) and ask for the names of members in your area who do residential work. Or look up registered architects in the Yellow Pages of your telephone book. Call those who are nearby and tell them your problem. Even if an architect cannot take on the job, chances are he can recommend someone who will be interested.

Make a rough floor plan of your house with dimensions and take it, and photographs of the exterior and rooms involved, when you go to talk to the architect. He may be able to show you in a rough sketch the best solution — perhaps one you have never thought of — to your problem. It would be even better if you drew your own design and asked him to criticize it and make suggestions. This is a good way to indicate to him what you have in mind and the scope of the work.

An architect will not charge you for a brief discussion, but if he spends much time giving you ideas or sketches, do not expect him to work for nothing. Ask first, and also ask who the best contractors and subcontractors are for the work you need done. He will know because he will have worked with many of them before and can tell you who is reliable and who is not.

If you are going to do all the work yourself, perhaps all you need from the architect is a quick sketch and advice on materials to get you started in the right direction. If more work is required, he will frankly discuss his fee and what you will get for it.

An architect's fee is usually a percentage of the cost of the work, but it can also be a set amount established in advance. On small jobs where you are going to do the work yourself, he can do the design for you, charging by the hour, with the contract consisting of a simple letter of agreement.

The Contractor

You will probably not need a general contractor unless the recreation room involves a number of trades and extensive remodeling. If you have an architect, ask him if, between you, you cannot schedule the work and supervise the various subcontractors.

If you do not have an architect and cannot do the work yourself, finding a good contractor can take months. You can call local architects and ask them for recommendations, but they will probably be reluctant to give you the names of their best men since good contractors are hard to find and are booked up long in advance. It is better to compile a list of several possible contractors and ask architects which one they think would do the best job.

It is a waste of time to check on a contractor or subcontractor with the Better Business Bureau. They can only tell you if any complaints have been lodged against any of their members, but joining the Bureau is hardly compulsory. The same is usually true of lumberyards and building supply companies. They depend mainly on contractors for their business, so you are not likely to hear anything bad about a contractor from them.

Banks and building departments can be good sources of reference, but they usually refrain from unfavorable comments for fear of offending someone or of becoming involved. The recommendations of friends and an excellent local reputation are probably the best criteria for hiring a contractor you can trust.

Once you have found several contractors you believe can do the work, give them all identical sketches and specifications and let each one know that you are getting estimates from other contractors. If after you get back several bids the contractor you like the most has bid on the high side, ask him if he cannot meet one of the more reasonable bids. You may be able to work out an agreement.

Have a contract drawn up by your lawyer that includes the specifications and the dated sketch you gave the contractor for his bid. Also include in the contract under a "time is of the essence" clause the date the work will begin and when it will be finished. Agree to nothing verbally.

Working with a Contractor

Before signing the contract, ask the contractor for a work schedule and include it in the terms of the written agreement. The schedule will show when the workmen are to arrive, what they will be doing, and when the plumbing or electricity will be turned off so you can make other arrangements.

Do not follow the contractor or his men around asking questions or making changes in the plans. Keep children and pets away from the workmen and never ask them to answer the telephone or keep an eye on the youngsters while you run into town.

Pay the contractor according to the contract — only for labor that has been completed and materials that have been installed. Make the final payment only after the work is completed to your satisfaction. Once he has been paid, the contractor will seldom return to fix defective work.

Subcontractors

If you cannot find a contractor you can trust, you can have your recreation room built by hiring the subcontractors yourself. You can save money this way, but you may not be able to get the work done as quickly because the subcontractors will have to schedule your work in between the larger jobs they have with general contractors and builders. Since they depend on them for work consistently but may only work for you once, this is to be expected.

If you are going to act as your own contractor, the best place to start is with a good carpenter — unless, of course, you are going to do the carpentry yourself. Good carpenters are even harder to find than good contractors, and they are expensive, but worth it. Carpenters will have worked with the other trades you will need; therefore they will know the best men for the jobs you want done, and you can coordinate the schedules. Do not hire a carpenter as an employee or you will be responsible for withholding taxes and paying unemployment and workmen's compensation insurance. Draw up a written agreement with him, as with the other subcontractors.

If you decide to do the carpentry yourself, you will have to locate the other trades you need, using the process of bids and elimination.

Talk to your insurance agent to be sure you are fully covered in case of an accident. And when the recreation room is completed, be sure to increase your insurance to cover the improvement on your home.

Deed Restrictions

A deed restriction is a condition written into the deed to your property to protect you and your neighbors from unwanted alterations and to maintain a level of continuity in the neighborhood. Deed restrictions can supersede zoning ordinances, so you should reread your deed carefully before you alter the exterior of your house or add to it to provide space for a recreation room.

You may be prohibited from adding a room or from building an addition in a certain area. Building restrictions in the deed may state that any additions to the house must be of brick construction or that they may not have a flat roof.

Deed restrictions are designed to maintain the character of the neighborhood. They can be dogmatic, but with proper interpretation they can bring about better neighborhoods with stabilized property values.

Zoning Ordinances

Zoning ordinances restrict and define the use of land and buildings for residential, industrial, and business purposes. Unlike deed restrictions, these ordinances are almost always written for your protection as a property owner. They guard you against having the property across the street turned into a motel, a next-door neighbor building right up to your property line, or anything that would detract from the value of your house as a residence.

To determine if you are permitted to add to the house to create space for a recreation room, you must examine the plot plan or survey of your property. The lot line establishes the outer boundaries of the site, and within this lot line is a building line determined by the setback regulations in the zoning ordinance. Enclosed living areas must be constructed within the building line, but very often you are permitted to encroach on the building line by several feet if the construction is cantilevered over the foundation.

The zoning ordinance is usually available at your town hall or building inspector's office, so get a copy and familiarize yourself with it before you begin planning. These ordinances can be enforced by fines and the illegal construction removed if a variance was not obtained beforehand.

Variance

If you feel that you are being too tightly restricted by a particular zoning ordinance, you can apply to the zoning board for a variance. If, for instance, the zoning calls for a side yard at least 15 feet from the lot line, but the recreation room you want to add will leave a side yard of only 13 feet, you may apply for a variance. The zoning board of appeals meets periodically to review just such cases. After you announce your intentions to your neighbors, your application will come before the board and a public meeting will be called. Anyone objecting to what you are planning to do will be given a chance to voice that objection at the meeting. However, a solution is usually worked out to everyone's satisfaction.

Building Codes

The building code is designed to guarantee minimum safety standards, and will stipulate the minimum size of columns and beams that are needed to support a roof, the size and depth of footings, and so forth. It can also control the design of roofs so they do not collapse under a snow load or blow off in a high wind. The plumbing and electrical work are also governed by the code to protect your health and to protect you from electrical fires and shock. If you are required to obtain a building permit, the construction will be checked by a building inspector as the work progresses to insure it conforms to the code.

Building Permit

Often it is difficult to know whether you need a building permit. Usually none is required if all the work is being done on the interior of the house and there is no structural work involved. However, if the work will alter the exterior of the house structurally, you will probably need a permit. Building a pavilion at the rear of the house for use as a recreation room would require a permit.

Whether or not you do require a building permit will depend on the regulations in effect in your area, so consult the building department in your town hall. If you do need a permit, the fee will be based on the estimated cost of the construction. The issuance of a building permit will almost always assure you of an increased property tax the following year, reflecting the improvement in your house and property.

3
How to Do Remodeling and Finishing Yourself

Once you have a design and plan for the recreation room you want, the rest is largely a matter of manual labor, if you are familiar enough with construction to do the work yourself. Converting existing space into a recreation room amounts to more than putting up a partition with a door in it. You may want to hide pipes or heating ducts, add closets, a bar, or a new window with a window seat. If your existing space is not adequate, you can expand the area either by cantilevering over the foundation for a few feet or by building new space from the ground up.

Some of the structural work you may have to have done for you. It is the finishing — the paneling, trim, sanding, painting, varnishing, and tile work — that takes the most time and is the most expensive when you have to hire someone to do it, but this is the simplest and least demanding work to do yourself, requiring few tools and very little experience.

Reinforced concrete, built-up roofs, basic electric, plumbing, heating, and framing work are the most difficult phases of construction, but only some experience and the proper tools and equipment make even these tasks possible. The use of power tools, especially an electric circular handsaw, will make cutting lumber and plywood much easier and certainly quicker. However, when used carelessly, power tools can be extremely dangerous and the actual time you save using them on small jobs instead of a good handsaw can be accounted for in minutes. A saving not worth it when weighed against the loss of a finger, a leg, or a life.

Partitions

Partitions simply divide space and carry no load except their own weight; in contrast, a bearing or structural wall supports roofs and loads from floors overhead. All exterior walls are bearing walls, and usually there is one interior wall running the length of the house that is structural and supports loads from roof to basement or crawl space.

A partition has two parts, structure and finish. The structure usually consists of 2-by-4-inch pieces of lumber and the finish is either gypsum (plaster)

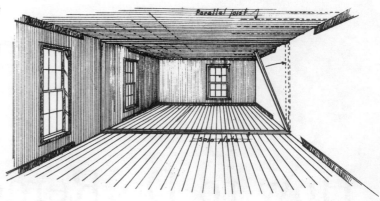

Beginning a partition. When ceiling joist runs parallel to the partition, as on the right, the partition must be directly underneath so it can be nailed to a joist. The end 2-by-4s should be wedged in and nailed to existing studs.

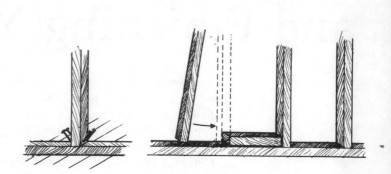

Studs are toenailed (right) to the plates on the floor and ceiling.

Wedge studs between the plates (far right) and use a spacer to hold the 2-by-4 temporarily as it is being toenailed.

board or some sort of paneling plus the trim. The 2-by-4s set vertically are called studs, the one used horizontally at the floor is called a sole plate, and the one used against the ceiling is called a top plate, even though before they get nailed down they are all 2-by-4s.

They do not actually measure 2 inches by 4 inches; these are rather, the widths set for the saws in the lumber mill. By the time the lumber is cut and dressed, the dimensions are closer to 1⅝ inches by 3⅝ inches, or sometimes 1½ inches by 3½ inches.

When houses are first constructed, the partitions are made flat on the floor and then raised into position. You cannot do that on an existing house because the edges of the sole and top plates would not permit them to be raised to a perpendicular position, and since floors and ceilings are rarely level, there could be large gaps left at the ceiling.

Building Partitions

To begin, remove the trim next to the floor and ceiling on the walls the partition will butt into so a stud can be placed flat against the walls. If the partition is to run parallel to the ceiling joist, it must be placed directly under a joist so the top plate can be nailed to it.

Using a metal carpenter's square (an L-shaped ruler), draw the exact location of the partition on the floor, wall, and ceiling. Do not use a 2-by-4 to draw with because it will not be perfectly straight. Nail the first 2-by-4 to the floor, carrying it across any door openings. (These will have to be cut out later, but without this small waste, the wall can easily get out of kilter.) This is now the sole plate. If the partition is on a concrete floor, use special steel nails that penetrate masonry. Next, nail a 2-by-4 to the ceiling and be sure that it is nailed to the joist. This is the top plate.

Begin the vertical part of the partition by nailing a 2-by-4 against each wall. These are now studs. Studs are usually spaced 16 inches on center because most building products are manufactured in increments of 8, 16, 24, and 48 inches. Often a spacing of 24 inches is adequate on a partition.

Since the floor and ceiling are usually not level, each stud will have to be measured and

Nail gypsum board to the studs, even if
paneling is to be the final finish, to
deaden the wall.

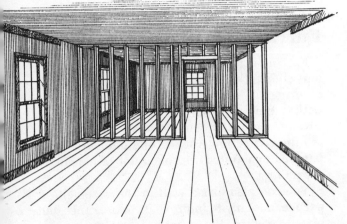

Place studs in the partition 16 inches on
center and double them around doors.

cut separately. They are held in place by toenailing them (nailing at an angle) to the sole and top plates. Wedge the stud into position — it should fit tightly between the plates on the floor and ceiling — and toenail it to the plates, using a precut piece of 2-by-4 to hold the stud in place while you are nailing it. Double the studs around door openings.

If convenience outlets and electrical switches are to be placed in the partition, they should be installed before the gypsum board or finish is applied, not only for ease of installation, but also so any wiring can be approved by a building inspector.

The wall finish can be gypsum board or paneling. Gypsum board is nothing more than plaster held together between two sheets of heavy paper. It is ⅜ inch or ½ inch thick, 4 feet wide and 8 feet long. To cut it, all you need is a knife that will hold a single-edge razor if you do not want to buy a standard, but inexpensive, Sheetrock knife. (Sheetrock is a brand name of gypsum board that has become universally used when referring to any brand.) You do not have to slice through the board; simply cut

through the paper on one side and it will break like a cracker along the split.

Nail it to the studs with 4-penny nails if it is ⅜ inch and 5-penny nails if it is ½ inch thick. Keep the nails at least ⅜ inches from the edge and a maximum of 7 inches apart. Use just enough force to slightly indent the paper without breaking it. The nail holes and joints are taped and spackled. (Spackle is a paste you squeeze over imperfections with a putty knife to hide them.)

If the wall finish is to be plywood paneling, apply the gypsum board anyway but don't bother to tape or spackle it. The additional thickness it gives to the wall will improve the sound-deadening qualities of the wall, which with only light paneling would have a drum-like effect on noise.

Nail and glue the paneling to the gypsum board. The edges of the paneling should fall on the center of a stud because the edges can warp away, exposing the interior of the wall. The nails are coated to blend into the paneling and need no additional finishing.

The trim at the floor, ceiling, and around the

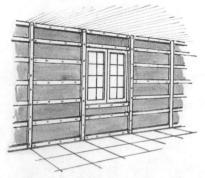

Furring strips around a window.

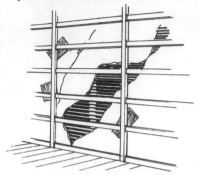

Furring can be used over damaged plaster.

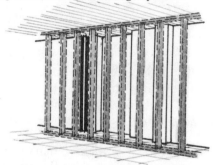

Furring over an uneven wall, pipes, and ducts.

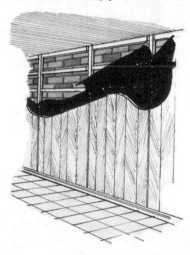

Tack building paper to furring strips between masonry and paneling to reduce damage from moisture.

door goes on next. Trim is a standard lumberyard item and can usually be bought to match the rest of the room.

Electric switch and outlet plates are the last things to go on the partition. Leave them off until after you paint and you will save a lot of time by not having to daub gingerly around them.

Furring a Wall

Furring is not, as one of my startled and anxious clients thought, mink-coating a wall. It is covering an existing wall, usually masonry, with a new wall surface. Furring is used to cover structurally sound walls with a surface too uneven or too cracked and damaged to be papered or painted without a lot of expensive repair first.

You can also furr a wall in the basement or garage, not only to improve its appearance, but also to retard the dampness by preventing moisture from condensing on the cold masonry wall. Be sure the dampness is caused only by condensation of normal moisture, or you could be covering over a serious problem that will cause difficulty later.

Strips of wood called furring strips are glued and nailed to the wall to provide a level anchorage. If the wall is uneven, the furring strips must be leveled with pieces of wood shingles called shims. If this is not done, there could be irregular joints in the gypsum board or paneling, which will produce a very unattractive wall. When the wall is to be insulated, you can use studs as furring strips and treat the wall as a standard partition.

Slight dampness on a masonry wall can be treated by painting the wall with a thick coat of white waterproof Medusa portland cement paint. You can also tack asphalt-coated building paper to the front of the furring strips to protect the plywood or gypsum board from moisture, which can damage both.

When there are a lot of pipes and electric cables and a number of small variations in the wall, it can be better and less expensive to furr the entire surface rather than try to cut and box around all the obstructions.

Place the furring strips around all doors and

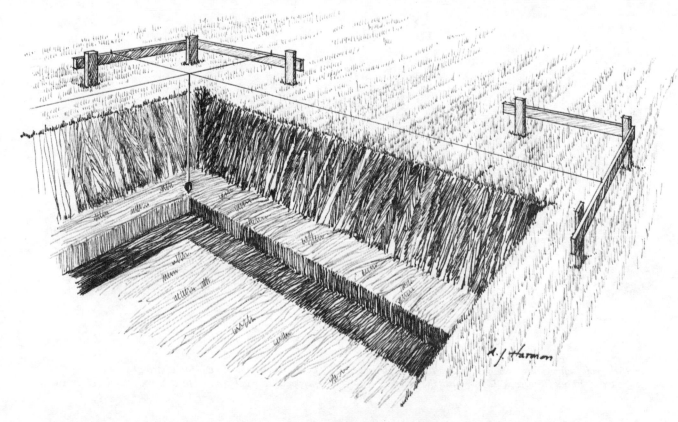

Stakes, batter boards, cord, and plum bob are used to fix exact location of footing and foundation walls.

windows, in the corners, and along the top and bottom of the wall. Continuous vertical strips should be placed every 4 feet on center, and horizontal strips at intervals of 16 inches.

Gypsum board and paneling can be nailed directly to the furring strips. The trim and finish can then be completed.

Building a Footing

The foundation of a house consists of a foundation wall set on a footing. The footing is the very base of the foundation and is made of concrete poured on undisturbed soil. Small footings and foundation walls offer few problems if no hidden pipes, wells, old foundations, or other obstructions are uncovered.

Before digging into the ground, be sure that no plumbing, electrical, telephone, gas, or water lines are going to be encountered. In most areas of the country the footing is dug to a depth of 3 feet, but it should be at least 12 inches below the frost line. If it is not, water and moisture can freeze under the footing and lift it up, breaking the footing and wall. This will not necessarily bring the house crashing

down, but it will allow groundwater to flow freely into the basement.

When planning the addition to the house, use modular-size concrete block — width of 16 inches — to determine the size of the extension because it conforms to the stud placement of 16 inches. This will save a lot of cutting of both concrete block and plywood.

The tools you will need to build a concrete footing and concrete block foundation wall are the standard household tools such as a good hammer, a shovel, a hoe, and rolled steel measuring tape, plus a carpenter's square, a trowel, a mason's long level, a line level, a plumb bob, some strong cord, and some sturdy wooden stakes.

Begin by measuring the exact location of the outside of the foundation wall. You will need a 2-foot clearance on the ditch side of the wall to work freely. Mark this area off with the cord tied to the sticks securely hammered into the ground. Start digging along this line and excavate the entire area until you reach the depth of the top of the footing.

As a rule of thumb, the depth of a footing is equal to the width of the foundation wall, and

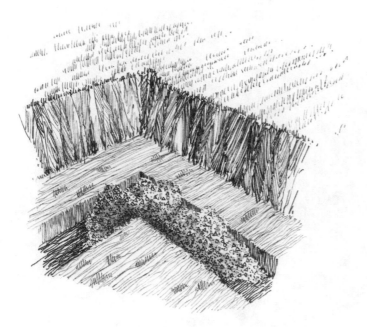

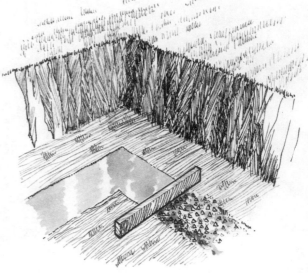

If the soil is firm, not loose and sandy, the concrete can be poured without formwork directly into the trench.

Level the concrete by moving a straight board perpendicularly back and forth across the top of the trench.

the width of the footing is twice that of the wall. Usually foundation walls are made of 8-inch-wide concrete blocks, so the footing will be 8 inches deep and 16 inches wide.

Mark off the exact location of the footing, using the sticks and cord. Unless the soil is very loose and sandy, the concrete for the footing can be poured directly into the trench. As you are digging the trench for the footing, keep the sides straight and the bottom as level as possible. If you do dig too deep in a spot or two, do not fill it in with soil because this may not support the footing. Leave the deeper spots as they are and fill with the concrete as it is being poured.

The most tiresome part of masonry work is mixing the concrete, so if the footing is going to require more than five or six bags of ready-mixed cement, it might be better to rent a portable concrete mixer so you can get through the pouring in one easy day.

There are many variations in concrete mixes, but usually for a footing the mix is one sack (which is equal to 1 cubic foot) of cement, 2½ cubic feet of sand, 3½ cubic feet of gravel,

and 5½ to 6¼ gallons of water, depending on how wet the sand is to begin with.

If you do not want to rent a mixer, you can use a metal wheelbarrow or make a large shallow box out of heavy scrap lumber and exterior plywood to mix the concrete in. You will need a shovel and a hoe. A square garden shovel is best, and a mason's hoe with two large holes in it will help you mix faster and easier. Whether using a mixer or mixing by hand, mix the cement and sand together first, then add the gravel. After these three have been mixed, add the water.

You can get the fresh concrete to the trench in a wheelbarrow or you can build a trough to direct it from the mixer to the footing location. The concrete should be poured and in place within a half hour after mixing.

After all this careful preparation, the concrete is rather unceremoniously dumped into the trench and spread around with the shovel. Level the final surface with a piece of straight lumber run perpendicularly back and forth across the top of the trench. The finished top of the footing does not need to be smooth, but it

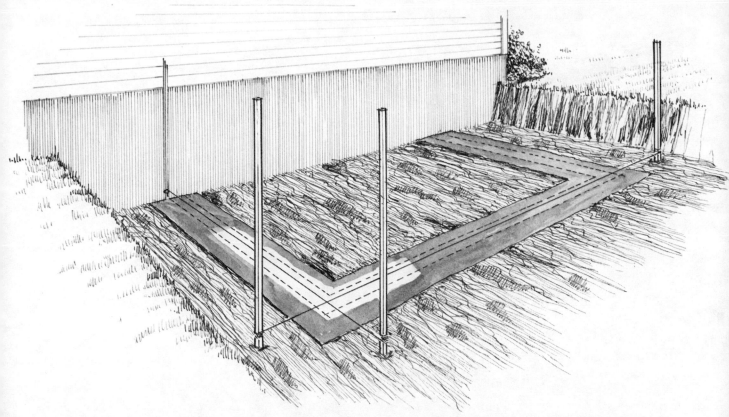

After the footing has cured for a few days, begin the foundation wall (dotted) by locating the outside line with stretched cord. The light section is where the mortar should be placed for the first row of block.

should be level. Small imperfections in the surface can be taken up by the mortar bed of the foundation wall.

After five to six hours, wash the surface of the footing with a fine spray from the hose. The slower the concrete dries (called curing), the stronger it will be. Allow the footing to cure for several days before continuing with the construction of the foundation wall.

To drain surface water away from the foundation — which you certainly should if the wall is high enough to provide basement space — lay terra-cotta drainpipe around the exterior of the footing on gravel. Cover the joints of the pipe with building paper and cover with more gravel.

The Foundation Wall

Building an 11-foot-high basement wall with drainage, waterproofing, reinforcing, and structural complications is probably too much for an inexperienced weekend handyman to tackle, but a 3- or 4-foot-high concrete block wall to support a small addition is not much more complicated than children's blocks.

The Mortar

Most amateur masons will find it easiest to use packaged mortar, adding just enough water to bring it to a workable consistency. Do not make more than a bucket or two to start with because mortar begins to harden as soon as the water is added and cannot be used after an average of two hours. Once it has started to set, throw it out and make another batch.

You will not need a portable mixer for the mortar because, first of all, you will not be able to work fast enough to use up any great quantity, and second, you will have to experiment a little to get the consistency easiest for you to work with. Start by mixing the mortar in a clean bucket or wheelbarrow. Use the same container, whether it is an old beer can or a plastic bucket, to measure the parts.

If you do not use a packaged mix, the mortar mix for average conditions should consist of one part portland cement, one to two parts lime putty or hydrated lime, five to six parts sand, and just enough water to give the mixture the consistency of putty. The more lime you put in, the smoother it will be, but too much will make

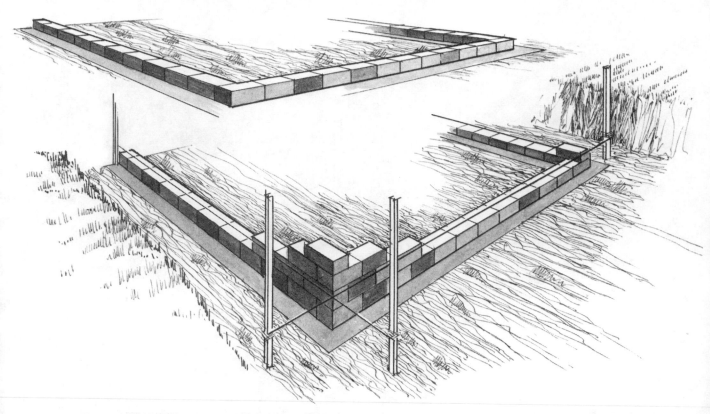

The first row of block must be straight and level. Begin the next rows at the corners, moving the cord up to level each row.

a weak mortar. Add only enough water to make the mixture easily workable yet firm. If, after a while, the mortar begins to get hard, do not try to add more water to make it workable because if you do, it will come out of the joints like graham cracker crumbs. However, the mortar is the last thing you do when you are laying a concrete block wall.

Building the Foundation Wall

Using the cord and the stakes, center the foundation wall on the footing and establish the outside line of the wall. Fix the stakes in the ground and tie the cord between them at the height of the top of the first course of block. Use the line level hanging from the cord to make sure the cord is tight and level. The stake will have to be as high as the top of the foundation wall is going to be because you must move the cord up and level it for every course of block.

Lay the blocks out along on the top of the footing, leaving ⅜ to ½ inch for the joints, to be sure the blocks come out even without cutting. Remove the blocks and spread a bed of mortar

on the top of the footing a bit wider than the wall is to be. Putting mortar on the footing for the first course and putting it on blocks or bricks that are about to be set into a wall is called buttering, probably because it goes on the block in about the same way as a lavish cook would butter bread.

Put down mortar about ½ to ¾ inch thick and furrow it with a trowel for a good setting bed. Lay the corner block first, following the string line for an accurate setting. Use the mason's level, resting on the top of the block, and tap the block until it is dead level and square. Butter the butt end of the next block and more or less ease it slowly into position so the mortar squishes into a joint.

Although the blocks are described as 8 inches high and 16 inches long, the actual dimensions will be ⅜ to ½ inch smaller to allow for the joints so that the wall comes out in even feet. For instance, a wall three blocks long with mortar in the joints should come out measuring exactly 4 feet.

Following the line established by the cord and using the mason's level to tap the blocks into alignment, lay the first course, starting at the corners for three or four blocks and working toward the center. Buttering several blocks at a time and setting them with the buttered side up will allow you to work faster.

Build up the corners next, stepping up three or four blocks and using the plumb bob for a perfectly vertical line at the corner. Put mortar on the inside and outside flange of the block already set, and on the two flanges of the end of the block. Tap each block into place.

Extra mortar that squeezes out of the joint can be scraped off the surface and reused, but if it falls on the ground, forget it. If the mortar slips off the block as you are setting it, remove the block and start over. Do not try to squish mortar into the joint after it has fallen off. This will create a weak joint.

As you will be working from the corners to the center of the wall, you will have one final closing block in each course. It is here that you will see how important it is to keep the joints of even size and the blocks carefully spaced and level.

The last block in the course should be buttered on both ends and slide in comfortably. If the blocks have been carelessly placed, the last block may not fit, having either too wide a joint, too narrow a joint, or no joint at all. It is better if the joint is a bit wide rather than a bit narrow because a too-narrow joint will not provide a good bond. If the joint is too small, you will have to knock some of the flange off with a hammer. This is not a disaster, but it is very hard work.

The crawl space will have to have air circulation to prevent the wood structure it supports from rotting. Metal vents, the same size as the block, should be inserted in each wall.

As you near the top of the wall, you will have to insert two anchor bolts at each corner and one every 8 feet on center in the run of the wall to secure the 2-by-6-inch wood plate to the block wall. Two blocks from the top of the wall, place window screen or stuff wadded-up newspaper into the block cavity at the locations of the anchor bolts. This will prevent the cement holding the anchor bolts in the wall from getting lost in the wall until it dries. When the top of the wall is reached, fill the cavities with mortar

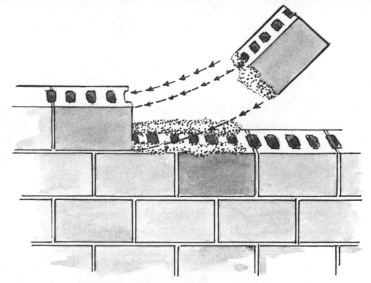

The blocks are buttered and set into place, using the motion shown.

Working from the corners, the last block should be buttered as shown and slide comfortably into place.

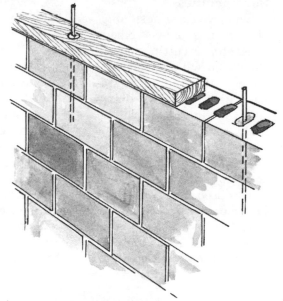

Anchor bolts are set in mortar and block cavities, to tie the plate and the wood structure to the foundation.

and sink ½-inch anchor bolts into them at the various locations. Leave 3 to 4 inches of the bolt exposed so the wood frame structure can be securely bolted to the foundation wall through the 2-by-6-inch plate.

Bars

Not every family wants a bar in their recreation room, but somehow when there is one there, people tend to gather around it to relax and talk. Before you start to build a bar, look at some that are on sale in furniture and department stores — not with the intention of copying them, but to get an idea of what you want.

If you are going to the effort of building a bar, do not make it a cute little thing that caves in the first time someone decides to sit on it instead of at it. It should be as strong and serviceable as a kitchen cabinet and as attractive as a dining room sideboard.

Most people make the mistake of building a bar that is too small. Allow 24 inches for each person who will be sitting or standing at it. This means that it should be at least 6 feet long because there is no point in building it for less than two couples — three people sitting and one bartender. This may seem large at first, but women often sit sidesaddle at a bar and not straight on as at a dining table.

Bar Facilities

When you are designing your bar, you can also include a beer dispenser, a sink, a refrigerator, a cutting board, and a back bar. It should go without saying that any bar for a home with children in it should be designed with a locked liquor cabinet.

If you like cold draft beer, you can either build in a commercial dispenser or provide space for a self-contained beer tap unit so you can move in a keg of beer for the occasional cookout or neighborhood bash. A self-contained unit is probably more practical because a regular dispenser must be wired for the refrigeration required, unless you are English and like your beer at room temperature (but even the English are giving up on that). A full keg is 25

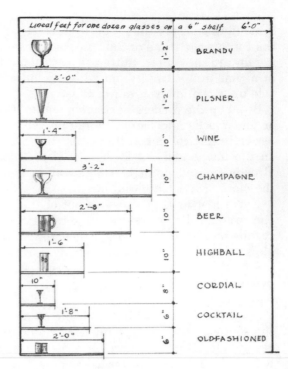

Storage space required for glassware.

inches high, 23 inches in diameter, and holds 496 8-ounce glasses of beer. A half-keg is 25 inches high and 17⅛ inches in diameter; a quarter-keg is 16½ inches high and 14½ inches in diameter. All you need is sufficient space in the bar, a sturdy reinforced shelf, and a hinged top.

Commercial beer dispensers come in many sizes, beginning as small as 1 foot 6 inches wide and 3 feet 6 inches high. A permanent installation may require a separate licensing permit from local authorities, so check the law in your area.

A small stainless-steel bar sink is an inexpensive and welcome addition to any bar, especially one that has a tap for beer because beer should not be poured into a dry glass. Bar sinks are manufactured as small as 1 foot 3 inches wide and fit into a standard 24-inch counter top. They are self-rimming and simply slide into the counter. In some cases you can get by with only a cold-water line if the kitchen is not too far away for washing glasses. The drain can be made of plastic, and although it will have to have the same trap and vent as any other, you

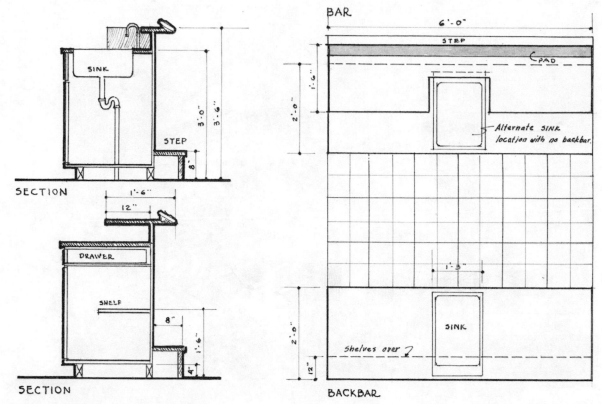

Recommended dimensions for an average bar.

can make standard plastic plumbing connections with only a saw and glue.

A bar that contains a sink and plumbing is called a "wet bar." One without a sink is a "dry bar," and if it is not nailed down to the floor, it is called a "portable bar."

A combination sink and small under-the-counter refrigerator is available in a number of designs. Some also include a built-in two-burner range top and come in sizes as small as 24 inches. Their price is about that of a regular refrigerator, and they are handy for everything from a quick cup of coffee to cooking and keeping things warm for a bar-served buffet.

You can include a small cutting board in the surface of the counter for slicing sandwiches or cutting fruit for old-fashioneds. Do not break up the surface of a small bar with a big cutting board. For appearance' sake it is better to keep it small unless you want to make the entire counter out of butcher block. This is very effective, but butcher block needs a lot of attention and is hard to keep clean because it should have no finish except vegetable oil.

You can design a cutting board to slide out over a drawer from under the counter. This does not have to be anything fancy and can be a clear pine board oiled with salad oil.

A back bar is a counter, cabinets, and shelves for glasses behind the bar itself. Unlike the back bar in commercial establishments, which is usually lined with mirrors and open glass shelves stacked with all sorts of tumblers, the back bar in a home is usually closed. Glasses set up on a home bar normally do not get enough use to keep them all glittering, and if on an open shelf would have to be washed before as well as after each use. For this reason, most people prefer standard kitchen wall cabinets. If the space under the wall cabinets is to be used for temporary bottle storage, leave a space of at least 16 inches between the wall cabinets and the top of the counter.

Shallow glass or wood shelves can be built against the wall, using shelf tracks and adjustable metal brackets. Simply screw the shelf track to the studs, using each screw hole and the screws provided for a secure anchorage. Slip the 4-inch to 12-inch brackets into the track. The spacing of the shelves can be

Bar and back bar, designed as recommended on page 23.

changed at any time by moving the brackets up or down. If you want glass shelves wider than 6 inches, use tempered glass or plastic so there will be no danger of them breaking.

Shelf track can be bought by the foot at almost any lumberyard, building supplier, or hardware store. Brackets to hold the shelves are always available at the same store.

If you want to enclose the shelves to keep the glasses clean, lightweight sliding plastic screens can be fitted into a track on the top of the counter and at the ceiling or soffit. Tempered glass could be used, but it weighs a great deal more and is harder to work with than plastic.

Sliding plastic doors will require no frame and holes can be drilled into them for attaching rollers so they slide easily. If liquor is to be stored behind the doors on the counter top under the first shelf, locks can be fitted to the plastic doors. Since no two people arrange their glassware the same way, transparent doors will permit guests to find what they are looking for without opening and closing several doors.

"To get your feet up," as the saying goes, you will need a step or footrail at the front of the bar. A step should be 8 inches high and at least 8 inches deep. If the floor is to be carpeted, you can carpet right over the step.

Metal footrails can also be used. These are either cantilevered out from the front of the bar or floor-mounted and held in place with a bracket horizontal to the bar.

The working surface of the bar will be 36 inches from the floor, the same as a standard kitchen base cabinet, and it should be built with the same toe space at the bottom. This will allow you to work comfortably behind the bar without scratching your shoes or the cabinet.

There is a second horizontal surface at the front of the bar that is 6 inches higher than the working surface and 18 to 24 inches wide. This not only hides the working surface, but also gives people a surface on which to rest their arms and a space to get their knees out of the way and be more comfortable.

As an added touch of comfort, you can upholster the front edge of the higher surface. This edge of the bar can be any size, but usually a 1-by-6-inch board braced at an angle of 15 to 20 degrees is satisfactory. After it is in place, glue or staple a strip of foam rubber or polyethylene foam the length of the bar to the two edges and the exposed side. You can buy foam rubber in many thicknesses at most fabric stores. In this case, a 1-inch-thick sheet is the thickest you can work with easily. You cut it by marking the size you need and then slicing through it with a sharp knife.

Cut a strip of vinyl leather wide enough to wrap around the padded board, leaving an extra inch at the top and bottom and 2 inches on each side. Using a lath or thin piece of soft wood, wrap the top edge of the vinyl around it and staple it to the lath the length of the bar. Place the vinyl with the attached lath on the bar and staple it to the underside of the padded board. Then wrap the vinyl tightly around the padding and staple it to the underside of the bottom of the board.

You will have to use a stapling gun when you are working with the foam and the vinyl because tacks concentrate the pressure in one small area, which can tear the vinyl. Also, the small spaces you will be working in are too difficult to reach with a hammer.

Closets

Closets are no more than a series of small partitions, and the construction is the same with the exception of the doors. The best doors to use are hinged, sliding, or bi-folding.

Hanging Closet Doors

To hang a hinged door, mark the hinge locations on the door and jamb (the side of the finished opening) after you are sure the door fits into the opening. To allow for swelling, leave about a 3/16-inch clearance on the top and sides, and more on the bottom, especially if the door is to swing over carpet or a rug. Flush doors should never be trimmed more than ½ inch on each side.

After you mark the hinge locations, chisel out the door and the jamb to the depth of the hinge. The door must be perfectly level or it will not close properly, but will drift open or closed and probably scar the floor.

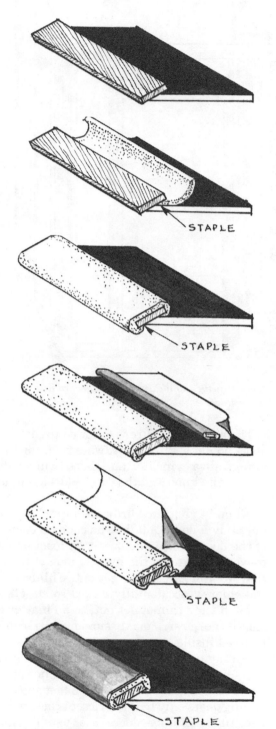

Stages for placement of padding and vinyl leather on the front elbow edge of the bar. Top to bottom, brace board for elbow rest on front of bar. Staple polyethylene foam to underside of board. Wrap foam tightly over board and staple to underside. Wrap vinyl around a thin strip of wood. Push wood strip and vinyl into foam and staple. Wrap vinyl around foam to underside and staple.

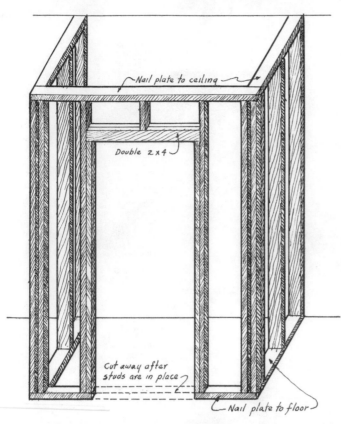

Basic structure for a closet with a standard height (6 feet 8 inches) door.

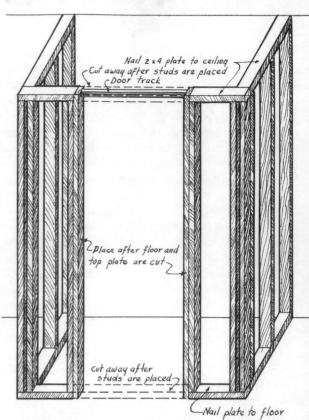

Basic structure for a closet with a ceiling height (8 feet) door.

The same procedure is followed to install the doorknob and catch. Hardware manufacturers almost always include templates to make drilling for the knob and the catch placement accurate.

When buying the hardware for a closet door, only buy a doorknob that has one on each side of the door, inside and out, or at least an easy-to-work release on the interior side of the door that a child can use to get out. Children (and the elderly) accidentally locked in closets will panic if they cannot get out, so no matter how small the closet, make sure no one can get trapped inside.

Sliding doors are much easier to hang than bi-folding and cost less, but should not be used on closet openings of less than 5 feet since with sliding doors only half the closet is accessible at one time. Sliding doors are usually either paneled or flush hollow-core doors. Hollow-core doors consist of two thin sheets of plywood glued to a frame. For this reason a maximum of ½ inch can be trimmed from the sides.

Design the opening carefully so that you do not have to trim the doors at all. The lum-beryard where you buy the doors and hardware can help you determine the height and hanging distance of the track and rollers.

To install the doors, screw the track to the underside of the door opening, using the holes provided in the metal track. Next, fasten two rollers either directly to the top of each door or on the side at the top, depending on the kind you buy.

The doors are simply lifted into place and the rollers settled into their tracks. Leveling screws in the roller hardware allow you to compensate for small errors in measuring and carpentry. Small stops are fastened to the floor to keep the doors sliding straight.

Bi-folding doors will open the entire closet to view, but the hardware, if not done with precision, can make them very cranky in operation. You can buy them prehung in a frame, and if you do, you should get them before you build the closet so that the frame becomes part of the construction.

These doors are mounted with a bearing assembly that allows them to slide back and forth in the track and open and close at the same

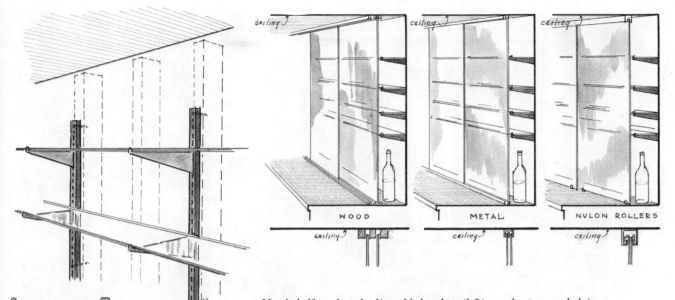

BRACKET 4" TO 12"

Screw shelf track to studs

Metal shelf track and adjustable brackets (left) supply storage shelving you can take with you when you move. Shelves can be hidden (right) by lockable and lightweight plastic doors that slide open on wood or metal rails or hang on nylon rollers which require no bottom rail.

time. The bearing assembly is fastened to the top of the door and mounted in the track before it is secured in the opening. The track and the door opening it is fastened to must be absolutely level or the doors will bind.

Both sliding and bi-folding doors can be bought to fit a floor-to-ceiling opening 8 feet high. The advantage to this opening height is that you can make better use of the space at the top of the closet and add shelves to the ceiling. With a standard door height of 6 feet 8 inches, a second or third shelf in the top of the closet would be practically inaccessible.

An 8-foot-high opening would also allow you to skip the construction, finish, and trim over the door opening. This will save time, but not much money because the taller doors are more expensive.

Closet Size

Most clothes closets are a minimum of 2 feet 4 inches deep, but there are recreation room items that are difficult to store in these, such as card tables and folding chairs. Few closets can take a 31-inch-square card table head on, and if

the table has to be stored parallel to the door, it will be hard to put away and remove because of other things in front of it.

A shallow closet 1 foot deep and 33 inches wide will hold three or four folded card tables. Folding chairs and hostess tables are 2 to 3 inches thick when folded, and these can be hung on the wall over the tables.

Shelving

The easiest, quickest, and if you rent or move a lot, least expensive shelving can be built in a matter of hours using the same metal shelf track and adjustable brackets that were described earlier for a bar. You can change it any time to suit your needs, and if you move, you can remove it and take it with you. If anything is nailed down in a house or an apartment, you are usually required by lease or law to leave it when you move.

The shelf track must be fastened to studs, which are not too difficult to find in frame construction. If the walls are concrete block or poured concrete, it will take more time, but you

Built-in twin couches with storage space in the base, upholstered with polyethylene foam and vinyl leather, using a stapling gun.

Architect, A. J. Harmon, A.I.A.

can anchor the shelf track anywhere and will not have to search for studs.

When the walls are of masonry, the simplest way to fasten the track is to mark the location of the screw holes in the metal track on the wall. Using a star drill (a masonry drill in which the point is in the shape of a star), make holes in the concrete block slightly larger in diameter and length than the screws that come with the track.

After the holes have been drilled, hammer wood pegs into them, using pegs that fit very tightly. You can then screw the shelf track into the wood and fasten it against the wall.

Basically the same principle is followed in fastening to concrete, and you may be able to use plastic inserts or lead cores instead of the wood plugs. However, concrete can be much more difficult to drill into, so you should probably insert a material that will hold the screws. If it becomes a problem, ask a mason for advice.

Window Seats and Dining Booths

Built-in seating is so much less expensive than conventional sofas and couches that it is surprising it is not used more often. One reason may be the exorbitant cost of upholstery, but there is a way to lick that. A built-in window seat can cost less than half what a sofa costs, even if you have to hire a carpenter to come in and build it for you. If all the materials are at hand, one carpenter should be able to build either a window seat or a booth in a day. Of course, if heating and wiring have to be moved, it will cost more, but usually they can stay where they are.

Finishing and upholstery will have to be done by the homeowner, but that is the easiest part, even if you do not sew.

If you are building a window seat over forced warm-air heating registers, build the seat far

Plywood and 2-by-4 construction of the couches shown in the photograph on the left. A dining booth is built the same way although the dimensions are closer to those shown on the next page.

enough out from the wall so the ducts can be extended to a shelf behind the back of the seat.

When the heating is done by hot-water registers, set metal grills in the shelf behind the seat back and in the toe space next to the floor in the front of the window seat. This will allow air to circulate through the seat over the radiator.

Constructing a Window Seat

Begin building the window seat by nailing the shorter width of one 2-by-4 to the floor, 4 inches back from the front of the seat, and another 2-by-4 to the wall. Brace these with a 2-by-4 on each end. Toenail 2-by-4s every 4 feet, extending the front 4 inches over the lowest one.

Nail a small piece of wood against the wall to support the back of the shelf. Nail vertical 2-by-4s to those spaced every 4 feet to support the front of the shelf and the back rest.

The finished height of the seat will be 15 inches, or sofa seat height, for a window seat, and 18 inches for a dining booth. If you are going to use 4-inch polyethylene foam, take that into account, along with the 1⅝-inch height of the 2-by-4 that will be nailed on top of the vertical 2-by-4s at the front of the seat.

Finish off the front of the seat with ½-inch-thick plywood or finishing lumber and cover the backrest and seat with ½-inch plywood. Keep the plywood 2 inches below the top of the finished backrest. If you plan to use the base of the seat for storage, cut the plywood for the seat 6 inches in front of the backrest so that when it is opened it can be leaned backward at an angle. That way it will not fall forward on your head when you are putting things in storage.

Polyethylene foam comes in standard thicknesses, but the lengths can vary from one manufacturer to another so you may want to

The base of the window seat opens to provide storage space.

take this into consideration when you are laying out the design of the seat. Trapezoid-shaped foam is available for the back cushions. The top of the back cushions should extend at least 2 inches over the plywood, and the front of the seat cushions should overhang an inch. Since my method of upholstery will compress the foam slightly, the lengths and widths should be a bit oversized. You can buy polyethylene foam at almost any fabric store.

When it is new, polyethylene foam is a very attractive white and it is a temptation to use it as it is. However, after being exposed to light and air, and especially sunshine, it soon begins to deteriorate, turn yellow and brittle, and give off a fine yellow dust. Therefore you should cover it as soon as possible.

If you can sew, you probably know how to upholster and do the piping around the edges of the back and seat cushions. I cannot, being an architect and not a tailor, but I can tell you how to upholster using a stapling gun — a job I find considerably easier than gift wrapping.

Upholstering, Harmon-style

You can cut the polyethylene foam like butter with a sharp butcher knife. Divide the back and seat into three or more sections, ¼ to ½ inch larger than the finished cushion is to be. Unequal pieces can be glued together. Cut ¼-inch plywood 2 inches smaller on all four sides than the cushion. What you are going to do is wrap the upholstery material around the foam and, with a stapling gun, staple it to the plywood on the back.

If you are covering the cushions with a fabric, the foam should first be covered with muslin or pieces of old sheet. If you are using vinyl with a corded back, you will not need a lining. A soft nubby fabric with a rubberized backing is the easiest to work with and will hide a number of errors in judgment.

Measure the front and sides of the cushion and cut the upholstery material generously enough to wrap around the cushion and cover the plywood back by at least 2 inches. Put the upholstery material flat on the floor with the outside down, lay the cushion on top, and center the plywood on the back of the cushion.

Wrap the material over the top to meet the plywood and staple it to the plywood in the center of the edge. Do the same thing at the center of the bottom. Do not pull the material so taut that it bulges, but do make sure it is tightly stretched. Work from the center out, stapling every inch or so until you get to within 4 inches of the corner. Begin the sides by stapling at the center of each side and work to the corners. If the material is delicate, fold it over so the tension will not tear it away from the plywood.

Now comes the hard part, the corners. If you are working with a rough-textured fabric, you can just inch around the corners and the little tucks will not show on the front side. If you are working with vinyl, you will have to decide what kind of hospital corner you want. It is important that you use the same fold on all the corners. I prefer a 45-degree fold-back because it gets lost between the cushions when they are in place.

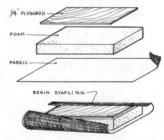

Quick and simple upholstery using plywood and a stapling gun.

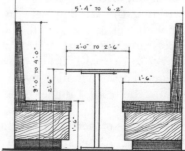

Dimensions for a dining booth. The height and thickness of the seat backs can vary to suit special needs.

4
Money — Where to Invest, How to Borrow

A recreation room is usually the last thing to be included in a home, and this is only naturally so. People are most concerned about having enough bedrooms, a kitchen that works, and another bathroom. However, with the rising cost of everything from gasoline to hamburger to greens fees, people are spending more leisure time at home and they want to spend it in an atmosphere as comfortable and imaginative as possible. And they do not want to spend any more money than they have to to get such an atmosphere.

Whether you are adding a room to the house, building a separate structure, or thinking about converting the basement, attic, or some other room into space for recreational purposes, start with the best plan and design you can devise or have made for you and then stick to it. This is especially true if you are going to do the work a step at a time. Each step should be complete in itself and also be an integrated part of the final design.

Spending

Only the wealthy can afford to change their minds and have things done over if they are not satisfied with the first results. If you do not know exactly what you want and where you want it and why, do not try to save money by avoiding professional help. It is better to pay an architect for a good design than to work for weeks finishing off the attic only to find that the ceiling is too low to be able to swing a Ping-Pong paddle or that the floor is not strong enough to support the billiard table you always wanted. Design is the most important element in every room of the house.

You can spend a lot of time and money on a recreation room then find that no one will use it because every time they do another member of the family complains about the noise. You can also underimprove the room so that when children are sent there to get them out of your hair, they feel as if they are being banished to Siberia.

It will cost a lot less if you do not have to change any of the structure, move windows and doors, or relocate plumbing and heating. However, if by doing any of these things you can improve the design, it is advisable to make the change. It is quite a mistake to be so in awe of a bit of plumbing that every time guests or the family want to go to the bathroom they have to navigate a flight of stairs, the kitchen, dining room, living room, and the bedroom hall.

After the design and the plan, the next best way to save money is by doing as much of the work yourself as you can. It is not wise to try to save money on electrical work by doing it yourself with a guidebook that has step-by-step instructions unless you have prior experience. You can kill yourself or burn down the house. You *can* save money by getting an experienced electrician's helper to do the work evenings or on his day off while you act as his helper.

If you have an electrical or plumbing problem you are not sure how to handle, ask an electrician or a plumber what to do about it. If he advises you not to tackle it, he might do it in his off-hours himself.

You can also save money on an addition by designing it in the modular units in which most building materials are manufactured. Concrete block is made just short of 16 inches long, and with mortar, three blocks come out to be 4 feet long. Studs are placed 16 inches on center, gypsum board and plywood are manufactured in 4-by-8-foot sheets that divide into exactly three 16-inch spaces. The less cutting of materials, the faster the construction and the least waste of material.

The worst way to try to save money is by falling for a sales pitch from a salesman working for an attic or basement improvement company who is canvassing the neighborhood looking for a basement to make into a showcase recreation room to illustrate his company's work. His crew will probably just be finishing a job in the next neighborhood, so he will promise you a special price because your house is so convenient to the equipment. Included in the fabulously low price will be free design consultation, free preliminary work, free waterproofing, a suspended acoustical tile ceiling, the company's own easy-payment financing, and a new $19.95 portable barbecue he just happens to have in his car — if you sign the contract he has with him now and make a small down payment of $100 to show your good faith.

The best that can come of this is for him to disappear after you have paid $100 for a $19.95 barbecue. The worst that can happen is for him to go through with the deal.

Free preliminary work consists of two very fat men smelling of beer coming to your house with a tape measure. You will be several days getting their fingerprints off the wallpaper. Free design consultation will be a choice between black and green or black and red asphalt tile. Anything else is extra. The waterproofing will turn out to be a coat of powdered cement paint mixed with too much water. The suspended acoustical tile ceiling, all 81 square feet of it, will be suspended so low to avoid pipes and ducts that it will scrape your hat off. The company's "own" easy-payment finance plan will be a standard finance company loan at 18 percent, but since you are paying it back through the remodeling company, a carrying charge that brings it to 25 percent will be added. If you get behind in your payments, the company can simply confiscate your house — with the help of the local courts.

The Yellow Pages are full of basement and attic remodelers, but even most of those that are reputable know very little about design or how a room will affect the circulation, the facade, and any future changes you may want to make in your home.

Financing

Usually the best way to pay for a recreation room is in cash. However, this is not always feasible, and in some instances not quite the best way. Much depends on the current interest rates and where and how your money is presently invested. There are a number of other ways to pay for a recreation room, and how you finance it is also influenced by whether it is a new addition or a conversion of existing space.

The amount you can borrow will depend on your house, the changes that a recreation room will make in it, your income, and your credit. To get a loan from any reputable source of financing, you will need a complete set of plans and specifications.

Start looking for money at your own bank and then compare its loan rates and terms with those of other banks. Regulations, rates, and terms change regularly, as do different banks' lending policies. Following are some of the ways you can borrow money.

Home Improvement Loan

Home improvement loans are nonsecured loans, meaning that no liens are placed against the property or the improvement unless the loan goes into default. The bank may send a man to inspect your house, and then the new room when it is completed, to see if the money was spent in accordance with your agreement. At this writing, the interest rates vary from 8 to 12 percent on a government-controlled loan of $10,000 with up to ten years to pay. However, it is not likely that you will need that much for a recreation room unless you are doing extensive remodeling at the same time.

Mortgage Loan

If you do not have a mortgage on your home, you can apply to a bank for a straight mortgage loan. The interest rate is presently between 8 and 10 percent. The amount of the mortgage will depend on the property, the house, what you plan to add to it, and your financial situation. Unless a recreation room is going to double the value of your home (and few will), avoid taking out a mortgage. If you own your home free and clear, keep it that way.

Mortgage Refinancing

This very expensive way of financing can only be used if you already have a mortgage on your home. The old mortgage must be paid off and a new one drawn up, which will involve lawyer's fees, bank charges, and probably a higher interest rate than you have been paying. It is a highly questionable way of paying for a recreation room unless you are adding another bath and a new wing to the house.

FHA (Title 1) Loan

Next to paying cash, an FHA Title 1 Home Improvement Loan may be the best way to pay for a recreation room if it is a real contribution to your house. This is a loan that is taken out through a regular bank by people who can qualify. If your income is low and your financial situation such that a bank does not want to lend you money, the Federal Housing Agency can guarantee payment to the bank. The bank will then lend you the money without risk. However, not all banks will handle FHA loans, so you must find one that will. The maximum amount you can borrow currently is $2,500 with an interest rate of 9½ percent, which would be enough to finance the average room.

FHA (K) Loan

This is a different kind of FHA loan and is usually suitable for financing a new addition for a recreation room. K loans are available to those who can qualify for them at 6 percent interest for a minimum of $2,500 and a maximum of $10,000 with twenty years to pay. However, additional charges and fee payments as the work progresses raise the total cost of the loan.

Open-End Mortgage Loan

This kind of loan can be a good way of financing a new recreation room provided you have a mortgage that permits it. An open-end mortgage provides that you may borrow as much money from the bank as you have already paid on your mortgage. Your mortgage will then be increased by the amount borrowed, and the length of time the payments are to be made will be extended.

Personal Loan

These are loans made by commercial banks at interest rates that currently vary from 12 to 18 percent. The maximum you can borrow is $10,000 for a minimum of three years. In spite of the high interest rates, excellent credit and references are required.

Finance Company Loan

This type of loan is available to almost everyone and is usually used to buy automobiles, furniture, and television sets. You should not use such a loan to pay for a recreation room or anything else in your house because the interest rates are very high, usually 14 to 18 percent on a maximum loan of $2,500. High-pressure home improvement salesmen carry finance company forms with them, and will try to get you to sign them to pay for work the salesman wants you to let his company do for you. Never sign anything without having your lawyer or bank look it over first.

Credit Union Loan

If you belong to a credit union, it can be a good source of money to finance a recreation room. Credit union terms and rates are usually generous, although there is a limit to the amount you can borrow.

Insurance Company Loan

You may be able to borrow on your insurance to pay for a recreation room, although it is a very poor way to pay for it. In any loan, read the fine print and be aware of hidden costs, add-on charges, and the true interest you will be paying.

Even if your own bank will not give you a loan, someone will usually be glad to explain loans from other sources, so you should ask your bank's advice before signing any agreements if you do not have a lawyer.

5
The Basement
Recreation Room

The basement is not the worst place for a recreation room because it can contain a lot of space that would otherwise be wasted, but it is certainly not the best place in most cases. Simply because it is in the ground under the house, the basement is often depressing. The situation is aggravated by low ceilings, lack of sunlight, poor access and exit stairs, and dampness. Dampness is, of course, the worst problem of all because everything else can be corrected, even to lowering the floor for added ceiling height. But if the basement was not built to be dry and waterproof at the beginning, to make it so can be expensive and sometimes impossible.

Do beware of any product or salesman that says that with one quick coat of "miracle something or other" he can waterproof your basement in one day. Even reputable contractors using approved procedures will seldom guarantee a perfectly dry and damp-proof basement in all seasons of the year.

In order to have a damp-proof and waterproof basement, it has to have been built that way, with drain tile around the footings and membrane waterproofing of felt and asphalt on the footings and foundation walls. This will take care of surface water, but there are other reasons for a damp basement — a hydrostatic head, for instance. This is when water presses up through the floor because of a ground spring or a rising water table.

If you have a light dry basement with high ceilings, plenty of air circulation and sunlight, an entrance through an upstairs hall, and a second exit directly to the outdoors in case of fire, and if you do not mind noise from a basement recreation room filtering to the other rooms of the house, go ahead and make the recreation room in the basement. However, if the basement is the least bit damp, that will have to be corrected first.

Eliminating Dampness

A damp basement can be caused by outside water coming in through a crack or leak in the wall or seeping through the wall or floor because of poor drainage or a high water table, or it can be caused by condensation within the basement itself. Moisture can come from a washing machine, a dryer not vented to the

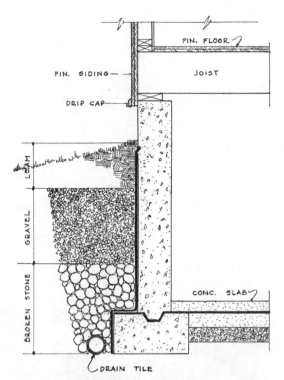

Basement waterproofing and drainage as it should be installed in frame construction.

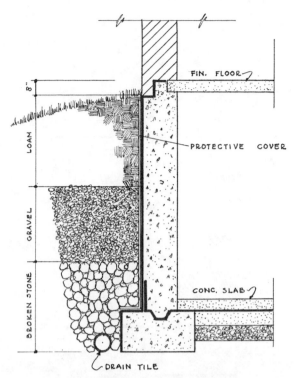

Membrane waterproofing as it should be installed in masonry construction where hydrostatic head is a problem.

1938684

exterior, a basement shower, or old clothing, books, magazines, and newspapers stored there. Throw out as much as you can.

Moisture in the basement could also come from leaking pipes. The leaks do not have to be large to cause problems. Just a hairline crack in a pipe or a connection can cause a constant drip, and once a wall or partition is damp, it will draw additional dampness to it.

A basement can be damp because of condensation forming on cold-water pipes and dripping onto the floor in the same manner that water forms on a cold beer glass. This is quite simply corrected by wrapping the cold-water pipes with insulation. Tape fiberglass insulation around the pipes or, for a neater better-looking job, use preformed pipe insulation that snaps around the pipe.

Condensation can also form in the same way when warm humid air comes into contact with the cool masonry walls of the basement. Very often this is mistaken for exterior water seeping through the basement wall, a condition that is difficult to correct. When the cause is interior condensation, it can be corrected either

by the use of a dehumidifier in the basement or by furring the masonry walls so the moist air does not come into contact with the wall.

If you live in a damp climate, tack tarpaper to the furring strips, leaving an overlap of 3 to 6 inches, before you apply the gypsum board or paneling. For extra protection of the paneling, paint the back before it is nailed to the furring strips.

Exterior water can make a basement very damp when it leaks through cracks in the wall, seeps through untreated walls, or comes up through the floor because of pressure caused by a high water table. These are all difficult and expensive problems to correct, although there are some external factors that can improve the condition.

Grade the soil away from the basement wall and make sure that gutters are clear so that water is carried to the leaders to be drained away and not allowed to overflow and run down the house walls. The leaders should carry the water away to dry wells or a storm sewer.

Do not allow the basement walls to become blanketed with ivy because it can grow

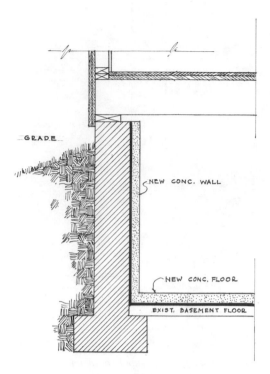

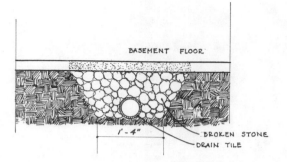

Drain tile placed in floor of existing basement.

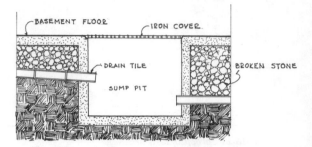

Drain tile and sump pit in floor of existing basement.

Waterproofing in an existing basement.

through small cracks, enlarging them. Keep the foundation planting within bounds and far enough from the house wall so air can circulate around the wall and through basement windows. If air can circulate around the house and through the basement, it will be dryer.

Quite serious is the water that gets into the basement through a crack in the foundation wall because of uneven settling that breaks the membrane waterproofing on the outside of the wall. This cannot be corrected until the settling has stopped. You can solve this problem only by removing the planting along the location of the break and digging a trench large enough for a man to get into to cement the crack closed and reapply the membrane.

Waterproofing

If the exterior was not waterproofed at the time of construction, with drainage tile set at the footing, this can be the only way for you to correct a damp basement. The work should not be attempted by an amateur and waterproofing a 30-by-50-foot basement can cost from $3,000 to $5,000. All the planting around the house must be removed and the basement walls and footing exposed so they can be cleaned and coated with a layer of asphalt, a layer of fiberglass fabric or felt, and another layer of asphalt. Only use a reputable contractor who has been recommended by someone who has had a successful basement waterproofing job done by him.

The problem of a hydrostatic head (water pushing up through the floor) can only be corrected by using membrane waterproofing on the floor and a new reinforced concrete floor poured on top of that. This can be done in conjunction with the use of a sump pump with varying degrees of success, but it is not wise to undertake this type of waterproofing in the expectation of preparing space in the basement for a recreation room.

If the seepage is only mild, some damp basements can be waterproofed with basement waterproofing paints, but this is a strenuous job that results in varying degrees of success. The 1976 Buying Guide issue of *Consumer Reports* listed 14 basement waterproofing paints, but recommended only one.

There are two types of waterproofing paints, one a powder to be mixed with water and used on wet surfaces, and the other a liquid to be used on dry surfaces. Both are difficult to mix, so have them mixed at your dealer's. Cracks in the wall will have to be filled with expanding cement and the wall cleaned and brushed according to the manufacturer's instructions on the can.

You will need to apply at least two coats of paint, and each must be put on with a brush rather than a roller to effectively cover the wall. It is expensive and you will need one gallon of the liquid type for every 60 square feet of cinder block and each 85 square feet of concrete. If you use the powdered type, you will need 10 pounds to cover 75 square feet of cinder block or 95 square feet of concrete. The powdered paints have cement in them, so they have to be used within a certain time after being mixed with water. Be sure to keep this in mind when having powdered paints mixed at your dealer's.

Windows and Doors

Light, especially sunlight, is the single most important element in any room, but particularly in the basement, where even the remembrance of sunlight from sometime during the day can help dispel an atmosphere of musty dampness. Doors let in light and fresh air, and provide a means of escape in an emergency. They also make the room more convenient to use for entertaining and for moving furniture in and out.

Cutting new openings for windows and doors in the exterior basement walls is not complicated if the masonry is concrete or cinder block so long as you remember that the plate anchored to the block and the structure above it must be supported. The situation is simplified if you place the new opening in a wall parallel to the run of the joist. In this case, the lintel, or horizontal support over the opening, need only be a double piece of lumber the same size as the joist.

The size of the lintel supporting joists perpendicular to it will depend on the span — the

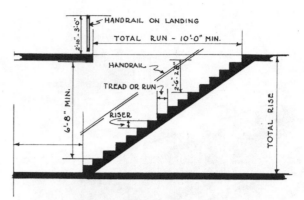

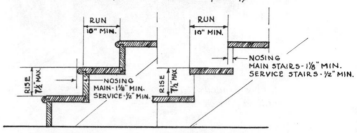

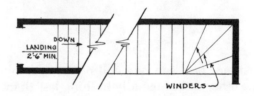

Stair construction for basements.

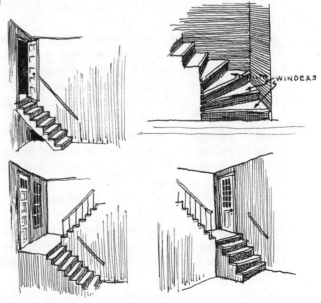

Dangerous stairs to be avoided.

Ribbon windows (left) for extra light and air in the basement. Metal and masonry light wells (right) can be excavated around individual basement windows.

distance between one end of the opening and the other — but usually nothing less than double 2-by-10s are used over a 3-foot door or window. You will have to use temporary support while the block is being cut away until the lintel is in place.

To cut the blocks, you will need a special steel chisel called a brick set and a short-handled medium-weight sledgehammer. Cut the opening in the masonry the size of the door plus the frame. At the top, where the lintel is to be placed, cut an extra half-block or 8 inches away to provide a setting base for the lintel.

Small basement windows of steel are sold in standard sizes to fit into block walls with a minimum of cutting. They are screened and open in from the top. Used singly in a large wall they are somewhat dreary, but you can combine them in a ribbon design when excavation for a larger window is not possible. But try to use a more imaginative window design than these.

If your house is located on a slope, you can remove the earth from the downhill side to a point where the footing will still be 3 feet below the frost line. This will open the wall for larger and more attractive windows.

Light Wells

For years, the light well has been a standard, if somewhat unimaginative, way of getting light and air into basements. However, if only a little thought is given to the design and placement of light wells, they can give any basement an exciting, almost conspiratory atmosphere. They do not have to be dark, stodgy little holes filled with last fall's leaves.

They can be large, deep, planted with flowers, and lighted at night. They can be run in series, and enclosed with glass, plastic bubbles, or open grills. They can also be left open with only a small curb and planting, or a decorative railing to keep stray dogs and children from falling into them. However, aside from what they can do for a basement, the most satisfactory thing about light wells is that they are easy to build.

Ribbon windows spanned by a bridge leading from the street to the front door allows light and air to enter the basement, overcoming the problem site.

A greatly enlarged light well provides a second exit from the basement while opening it to sunlight.

Building a Light Well

A light well is an excavated, walled, and drained area dug in the ground outside a window. Before you begin digging, make sure that you will not run into any obstructions such as electric, sewer, gas, or water lines.

First determine the size of the window. If you live in a cold part of the country, keep the bottom of the window 3 feet above the floor of the basement. The light well should be at least 2 feet longer than the window so there is 1-foot clearance on each side. There are no hard and fast rules for the width, but the face of the wall should be at least 2 feet away from the window to permit you to construct the retaining wall. The wider the well, of course, the more light and air you will get.

The retaining wall can be concrete block, brick, or a continuous piece of curved and corrugated aluminum or plastic. It does not have to be a wall at all; it could be made in the form of a rock garden sloped to the grade level and planted with flowers. Or, it could be railroad ties or creosoted lumber held to the slope with

heavy stakes also preserved with creosote.

Excavate the light well at least 12 inches below the level of the new windowsill. Trench a drain from the center, using 6-inch clay tile with the joints covered with building paper. Take the drain to a dry well 10 feet or more away from the foundation.

A dry well is just a large hole or an oil drum with the bottom removed, filled with large rocks or broken pieces of concrete block thrown loosely into it. Slope the floor of the light well to the drain and cover it and the drain tile with 4 to 6 inches of gravel. This will keep rainwater and melting snow from building up inside the light well.

If space is too tight to terrace the wall of the light well away from the window, concrete block is probably the best choice of material for the wall of the well. It is easy to work with and is constructed in the same way as the foundation wall. The block can also be painted to reflect light into the basement.

The quickest material to use for the light well retaining wall is corrugated aluminum or

A terrace off the basement, in the form of a sunken garden, also provides security for bedroom windows on the first floor.

plastic bent in a semicircle. The size of the light well will be restricted by the height and width of the material since horizontal joints are seldom satisfactory. Aluminum and plastic may be painted to reflect light, but both still tend to have a prefabricated appearance.

Regardless of the material used for the retaining wall, the excavation, drain, and gravel base will have to be constructed in much the same way. On a slope do not excavate deeper than necessary. When a vertical wall is used, tamp the soil down firmly behind it and grade it so that it drains away from the wall.

Soil has a natural inclination of 45 degrees, so if you want to slope the sides of the well to create a rock garden or terraces supported by creosoted plank, use this angle as the basis for the excavation.

Railroad ties can be used at a higher angle to form a steeper slope. Angle them to drain away from the light well, spike them together when one is used on top of another, and hold them in place with heavy creosoted stakes. Keep the soil 2 inches from the top of each tie and cover with ½ inch of gravel to keep mud from washing over the surface.

Finishing Floors

Paint is the quickest, easiest, and least expensive way of covering old concrete floors that are in fairly good condition, and it is surprisingly attractive and durable. A single color painted over the entire floor will make the room seem larger, but if it gets a lot of traffic it will show wear sooner than a floor painted in a pattern. A single color also has the disadvantage of revealing cracks, patched areas, and other imperfections. A floor painted in a pattern will draw your eye to the squares or stripes or whatever design you use, and paths worn in the paint will be easier to touch up.

If the old cement floor has to be patched up with new cement, wait six months before you paint it or the paint will not hold. Badly damaged concrete that cannot be patched can be covered over with cement.

Use a special cement paint or swimming pool paint for the floor. A roller is the quickest way to paint the floor for both the first and second coats if a single color is used. To paint the floor in a pattern, do the first coat over the whole floor with either a roller or a brush. After it dries (usually from several hours to a day), draw the squares, stripes, or pattern on the floor. Use a 1½- or 2-inch sash brush with the bristles cut at an angle to get neat corners and straight lines. Paint the outside of the pattern first; then fill in the center of each square or stripe as you go along.

There are some floor finishes that you should not use in a basement. Among these are linoleum, rubber tile, cork, cork-and-vinyl tile, roto-vinyl, some cushion vinyl, and some tile and carpet tile with self-stick backing. While the surface material may hold up when used below grade, the foam back and self-stick glue will not.

Asphalt tile, vinyl asbestos, and vinyl tile can be used below grade, and, with mastic, placed directly on concrete. When the concrete is in very poor condition, you can build a new floor surface using sleepers, 2-by-4s fastened to the floor with concrete nails every 12 inches, with a new subfloor of ½-inch plywood on top of them.

Asphalt tile is the cheapest tile you can put down yourself. Dampness will not affect it, but it stains easily, is brittle, and is very difficult to maintain. Imperfections from uneven surfaces underneath will show through, though not as much as they will with vinyl asbestos.

Vinyl asbestos tile is inexpensive, resistant to grease, and easy to clean, but it mirrors even slight imperfections from the surface on which it is placed. It also shows indentations from chair and table legs that you can never get out.

Vinyl tile is the most expensive and is available in several grades and thicknesses. It is no more difficult to put down than the cheapest asphalt or vinyl asbestos. It will show indentations and mirror some imperfections from underneath, depending on its quality, but not as much as vinyl asbestos. It is easy to clean, wears very well, and is resistant to almost everything except sharp indentations.

Walls

Dry basement masonry walls can simply be painted, or furred out and finished with gypsum board, paneling, paper, vinyl cloth, vinyl finished hardboard, grasscloth, or burlap.

The advantage of grasscloth, burlap, some of

Excavating under an existing house to build a basement in the crawl space area.

After the crawl space has been converted into a basement, lawn and foundation planting are replaced.

Every basement should have a second exit, even if it has to be as ugly as this hatchway stair.

the dull-finished textured vinyls, and other fabrics is that they can be applied over gypsum board without spackling the gypsum board. There are instances where you may want to tape it, but this is only a matter of running tape over the joints. On any smooth or metallic paper these joints would show through, but textures such as burlap will hide all sorts of cracks and imperfections. Cloth will also help deaden the sound in a recreation room.

Cloth is easier to hang than paper because the paste is applied to the wall. Begin by following a plumb line a few feet away from the corner, since a joint in the corner is too difficult to make. Cut the cloth squarely across the top and the bottom, fastening drafting tape to it to prevent raveling. On loose-weave cloth like burlap, pull a cross thread and cut along that line to get it square.

In the area where the first strip of cloth will go, cover the wall with the paste. Hold the top of the cloth by the drafting tape and press it against the wall at the ceiling. Carefully following the plumb line, work down the wall, smoothing the fabric against the wall with a rolling pin. Do not press it with your hands or you will squish it into imperfections and cracks. Butt the next length to the first.

With a razor cut off small threads and overlappings at the baseboard. If the joint between the ceiling comes out messier than you planned, it can be covered up with molding — but paint it before you nail it up.

Ceilings

Basement ceilings are usually a clutter of pipes and heating ducts. These obstacles, combined with the already low height of the ceiling, usually make a suspended ceiling out of the question. Suspended or hung ceilings are more suitable in garages, which have high ceilings free of pipes and other obstructions.

First-floor joists in the basement ceiling are usually 16 inches on center. Gypsum board can be nailed directly to them. Pipes and ducts can be boxed around, using ½-inch plywood or boards, so as to drop the headroom in as few places as possible.

Expensive, rigid styrofoam insulation can be placed between the joists and held in place with small strips of molding. It can be pushed against any flooring nails that have come through the subfloor. This will not only hide the nails and finish the ceiling, but also help keep sound generated in the recreation room from penetrating to the first floor. Some plastic materials, such as polyethylene, are highly inflammable and should not be used.

Acoustical tile, stapled to 1-by-3-inch furring strips, can also be used. It, too, is nailed, clipped, or glued, and comes in various sizes from 12 inches square to 12-by-32-inches long. Some of the larger sizes have a tendency to sag in the middle after a time. Buy only fireproof material.

6
The Attic
Recreation Room

There are a number of things to check on before you consider making a recreation room in the attic. First, make sure you have an attic. If there is only a trap door that lets you into a space between the roof and the ceiling, chances are that the roof structure is truss-supported. Several kinds of prefabricated trusses can be used, but the most common is the "pitched truss." Trusses are made of light wood and are usually spaced 2 feet on center. If your roof structure is made of these, you cannot consider using the space for a room of any kind because the lower members of the these trusses were not designed to carry any superimposed loads. Cutting or removing the diagonal members can cause the roof to collapse.

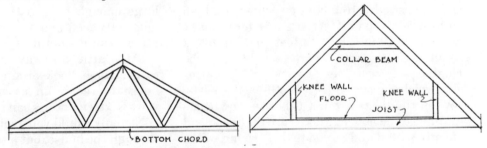

A prefabricated truss (left) and conventional attic structure (right).

If you have a roof structure that was built on site, check the distance between the collar beams and the top of the floor joists. A collar beam is a horizontal brace between the rafters, up about two-thirds the distance between the floor joist and the ridge. If this distance is less than 7 feet 6 inches, the attic space is not suitable for a room, and if made into one, may even be illegal since most building codes require all living areas to have a minimum ceiling height of 7 feet 6 inches.

Next, see if the floor joists are strong enough to support furniture and people. Many attics were not designed to be used as living areas. This can be especially true if there is no floor in the attic and only a few boards resting on the joist that may have been used to walk on when the insulation was installed. Since shorter lengths of lumber are cheaper to buy than pieces long enough

Plastic skylights are delivered with a protective paper covering.

to go from one side of the house to the other, most houses have floor joists that go from the outside wall to a bearing partition in or about the middle of the attic. At times these are only 2-by-4s that cannot support any weight except the gypsum board of the ceiling below.

If the joists are 16 inches on center, a 2-by-6 can be used to span 8 feet, a 2-by-8 for up to 11 feet, a 2-by-10 for up to 14 feet, and a 2-by-12 for up to 16 feet. There should also be bridging — crisscrosses of wood and metal or solid wood — every 8 feet to stiffen the joists.

When the joists are not this size, new joists will have to be added. Make sure that each end is firmly seated and nailed to the bearing walls. Nail the new joists to the existing joist every 12 inches, using 3½-inch nails.

Stairs

Also check the location and construction of the attic stairs. The stairs should be accessible through a hallway and not through another room. They should be convenient and easy to climb, with low risers and no winders. There should be a handrail on each side that will not pull away from the wall and is sturdy enough to take the weight if someone should fall against it.

The stairs should be quiet. The kind that squeak and make every footfall sound like a drumroll are probably constructed of thin boards with structural support that would not be able to handle the traffic to and from a recreation room. The stairs should be strong and large enough to hold the combined weight of four hefty men and a piano — a distinct recreation room possibility.

If the attic stairway has faults too difficult to overcome, look around the outside of the house to see if an exterior stairway might work. Exterior stairs can be a wise investment.

Not only would you avoid a lot of traffic going through the house, but a second exit would be a safety factor in an emergency when a number of people are using the room at the same time.

Insulating the Attic

Of all the tasks involved in making an attic recreation room, insulating the roof is the easiest, if not the most pleasant. All you have to do is staple light sections of mineral wool batts between the rafters of the roof and between the vertical studs on the outside wall. It is unpleasant because fine particles of mineral wool can get into your skin, hair, eyes, and lungs and severely irritate any part of you they

Protective covering should be removed only after skylight is installed and adjacent work is completed.

touch. Wear coveralls, gloves, a hat, and a face mask when you handle mineral wool.

You buy batt insulation in rolls 8 feet long and usually 16 inches wide to fit between standard stud placement, although other widths are available. Cut the outside paper envelope with a razor or gypsum board knife and cut through the mineral wool at the same time. Tearing it only scatters the tiny particles around.

Never use any form of insulation that is not fireproof (fire-resistant is *not* sufficient), waterproof, and vermin- and rot-proof. Using materials that do not meet these standards is dangerous, and worse than no insulation at all.

Insulating batts usually have a vapor barrier on one side. This should face the interior of the room when applied. Aluminum foil can be used on the inner side of batting to reflect heat back into the room, or if you live in a hot climate, on the other side of the batt, away from the room, to reflect heat out of the house and to reduce the cost of air conditioning.

Skylights

Unless the roof leaks, attics are rarely damp, but light and air are just as important in an attic recreation room as they are in a base-

ment. Usually the end wall will have a window in it, but for cross circulation you will probably have to add a ventilating skylight or a dormer.

Of the two, a skylight is less expensive because very little construction is required. A skylight that does not open, however, can allow an enormous amount of heat to build up in the attic, especially if it is on the south side of the roof. A skylight on the south side of the roof will help heat the attic in the winter, but it must be constructed to be opened in the summer to allow the heat to escape.

Skylights can be either clear double plastic bubbles with an air space for insulation, flat insulated translucent plastic, single clear plastic sheet or bubble, or single or insulated clear glass. If you use glass, never use anything except tempered glass so that if it should break, it will shatter into tiny harmless pieces and not large jagged chunks.

Since there is little construction involved, a skylight can usually be installed in an afternoon. It is run right over the rafters without cutting them. Most plastic bubble skylights are sold with an integral curb and metal flashing. Some, which are not screened and cannot be opened, are available with electric fans that pump the warm air out, but these are more expensive and require an electrical connection.

Various types of dormers can be built into roofs to let light and air into an attic.

The flat translucent type come mounted in a metal frame, but the curb and flashing must be done on the job. Both flat and bubble types depend on the rain to clean them and you should avoid any attempt to clean them on your own. Touched only once with anything, they are scratched for good. They arrive from the factory with a protective coating of heavy paper. Open the packaging and check them out when they arrive and if they are dirty or marred when delivered, do not accept them. If they are okay, rewrap them to keep them safe until the installation is complete.

Plastic is of much lighter weight than glass, and is easier to handle and work with, which is its main advantage. However, some companies' plastic bubbles have an alarming tendency to discolor and fall apart within a few years. Buy only from a reputable company and get a written guarantee from the manufacturer.

Dormers

Dormers will not only provide light and air, but will also increase the usable floor space in the attic. Shed dormers can expand the floor space by 50 percent, and they are the easiest and least expensive dormer to build. Shed dormers are usually begun at the third rafter from each gable end. The new outside wall can either be built flush with the wall below for maximum floor space, or it can be set back a distance. The latter method is more expensive because of the flashing required and you will lose some floor space, but it may be the one that looks better with the facade of your house.

You may only want to use a shed dormer on the back of your house and, because of the scale of your house, smaller doghouse or single-windowed shed dormers on the front. If you are including a bathroom with the recreation room, a small eyebrow dormer is inexpensive and better than no light or ventilation at all.

Use the same style of windows for the dormers as used on the other floors of the house so the dormer does not have a tacked-on look. Sliding glass doors can be used with a flush-shed dormer if it leads to a balcony or porch. Either will make cleaning windows on upper floors much easier.

An eyebrow dormer is inexpensive and better than nothing to let light and air into an attic room.

A single shed dormer is the least expensive type of dormer to build.

Balconies and Porches

Everyone likes balconies and porches off the upper floors of a house. They can be especially desirable off a recreation room where people will be irresistibly drawn to them for a breath of fresh air and a quiet escape after a heated Ping-Pong game. Parents will find them a comfortable retreat when chaperoning youngsters engaged in noisy games because they will permit them to supervise the activity without being in the center of it.

A porch can easily be expanded from a conventional stair landing and thus serve a dual purpose for very little additional money. Balconies do not lend themselves as well to doubling as stair landings because they cannot, unless especially designed, take the loads that may be required in accommodating heavy furniture and people.

Primarily, balconies should be narrow, 3 feet wide at the most, and well braced. They do not have the structural support of columns from the ground that porches have and are used mainly to protect and screen doors, to make

window washing easier, and to act as decorative elements on the facade. Of course, they will also shade lower windows and provide a sense of security for open doors leading to them, and they are excellent for sunbathing, for looking at the treetops, and for a quiet stroll or conversation.

Some metal companies and blacksmith shops can do metal designs of balconies for you, including the steel braces needed for support. However, most people prefer wood because of the ease with which it can be adapted to different conditions. Cypress is the best wood to use, but because of its scarcity, redwood is generally used (other woods can be substituted).

Do not butt the planks used for the floor, but leave a space of about an eighth of an inch between them. This will allow water to drain off and let air circulate around the wood to prevent it from rotting.

A porch off the recreation room will actually give you a second recreation space, and if stairs to the ground are included, a second exit. If the porch is not large, the joists can be held in joist hangers nailed to the studs against the house

A shed dormer can be recessed into the attic.   *A flush shed dormer increases attic floor space.*

wall and supported on the outer edge with a beam secured to columns resting on a square concrete footing.

The columns can be steel lally columns (4-inch round steel pipe). These present a much better appearance if the pipe is covered with nonstructural lumber and painted or stained.

The height of the railing is usually controlled by the local building department. A height of 3 feet is generally adequate, but lower heights may be acceptable and there are times when higher railings are preferred.

Finishing Walls

The attic walls can be finished in the same way as discussed in the chapter on basements, with the exception of cork. Cork is a very soft and handsome finish for a recreation room wall as long as it is not exposed to dampness. For this reason, it is not recommended for houses on the shore or by a lake. Cork should be placed over gypsum board (which will not need to be spackled since it will be covered), and it will help deaden the noise within the room and keep it from penetrating to other areas.

Cork is also recommended for the floor. However, if it is used for the floor, limit its application on the wall to one or two walls at most or it will become tiresome.

Flooring

Some of the floor finishes not recommended for basement floors, such as linoleum, rubber tile, and cushion vinyl, can work out very well in an attic recreation room. Roto-vinyl, however, is not recommended because it is not durable and most liquids, including water, will harm the design-printed felt. Asphalt tile, vinyl asbestos, and vinyl tile, which were recommended for the basement, will work equally well for the attic and have the same advantages and disadvantages.

Linoleum has been with us for years and is still a good floor covering. It is seamless, greaseproof, easy to clean, but not quite as durable as vinyl asbestos. Because it comes in such large sheets, it is not considered a do-it-yourself project to lay.

Rubber tile is still around. It wears well and does not show the permanent indentations of chair legs (as vinyl does), but it is very slippery when wet and needs constant attention.

Cushion vinyl can be an excellent choice for a recreation room. It is soft, will deaden sounds, and is seamless and easy to care for. But if the room is going to get hard use, such as roller skating, its wearing qualities are questionable. You should have it installed by a professional.

Wood, of course, can be used for the floor of an attic recreation room, but it is getting more expensive all the time. It is not that difficult to put down yourself, but then it must be sanded, stained, and varnished. Some of the new plastic-based finishes (sometimes called "bowling-alley" varnish) are easy to use and give a good hard tough surface that does not need to be waxed and is easily patched in areas of heavy wear.

Carpet is quiet. Whether or not it is suitable depends on how you plan to use the room. No one can keep track of all the different types, weaves, and combinations of synthetics and natural fibers carpeting comes in. You will just have to shop around and remember it is "buyer beware."

Any carpet will wear better and be softer and easier to clean if you use underpadding. Installation requires a professional, especially on stairs. Carpeted attic stairs are highly recommended even if you do not carpet the recreation room, because they are much quieter and safer than any other kind.

There are self-sticking carpet tiles, but these have a habit of becoming unstuck, particularly if you have a toddler or a playful puppy around the house. Before you buy any carpet, get a sample, put a match to it, and see how it burns. If it smolders and exudes toxic fumes, do not buy it. Some carpet burns very quickly and can spread a small fire all over your house within minutes.

An attic recreation room with high windows and a balcony over the collar beams provides a feeling of aery space.

Ceilings

The same things that were said of basement ceiling materials are true of attic ceilings, with the possible exception of a hung ceiling (see page 57). An attic has all that dramatic space under the gable; it seems a shame to cover it up.

There are so many humdrum 8-foot-high ceilings in our homes that when you have a chance to develop a space you should make the most of it. The space at the eaves, where the wall of the house and the roof come together, is not very useful. Some people want to try and develop this into storage, but it is complicated and expensive and a waste of time. If the room is used for living space, furniture will always be in front of it, and unless it can provide almost a full-height closet, you will have to crawl on your hands and knees to get to it.

Block the space off with a knee wall and run the ceiling right past the collar beams to the ridge. If the distance between the collar beams and the ridge is large enough to provide headroom, you can build an interior balcony along one side of the recreation room.

A hung ceiling under the collar beams will not save on heat because air goes right through the many loose joints. However, you will save a little on insulation and heat if you build a permanent ceiling at the collar beams. If you do block off the top of the attic, you will have to install vents in the opposite gables to prevent rot.

7
The Garage Recreation Room

An attached garage is ideal to convert into a recreation room. It has an entrance from the driveway, usually one from the kitchen and the rest of the house, and is probably on the side of the house away from the bedrooms and other quiet areas. In addition, it already has electricity, and most likely a hose bib or a water connection. Since it is on the ground floor, you can easily include a fireplace with an exterior grille backed up to it, and a porch or an enclosed courtyard for outdoor recreation and entertaining.

Since the garage is near or next to the kitchen, hot- and cold-water lines, and a soil pipe, you can include another bathroom and perhaps a wet bar, using the most economical connections. If you do, design the recreation room so that at a later date it can be made into a small apartment. It does not have to be an apartment that you rent, but it could provide comfortable living space for an elderly relative who likes to be on his or her own, but not isolated from the family.

Of course, the question that comes up here is: "But what will we do with the car?" The easiest answer is probably to build a carport. Carports are not as expensive to build as garages, but since they consist of only some columns and a roof, they do very little to protect the car except to keep the rain off. Carports on the front or side of the house, where they are most convenient to the street, still expose the car — and anything stored there that is not squirreled away in cabinets and locked closets — to view and give the house an unkempt appearance from the street.

If you live in a high-crime neighborhood, you will have to lock the car doors and leave lights on so the tires and hubcaps will be there in the morning. Other disadvantages are that building codes require that carports be built within the building line, and the space between the carport and the street is wasted. If security is not a problem, why not use this space to park the car, and instead of building a carport put the money into a porte cochere built over the entrance to protect you and guests from the rain as you get into the car? If you are worried about security, use the money to build a wall instead of a carport. The wall will not only help protect your property, it will also allow you to use your front lawn in privacy.

Replacing the old garage door with a bay window.

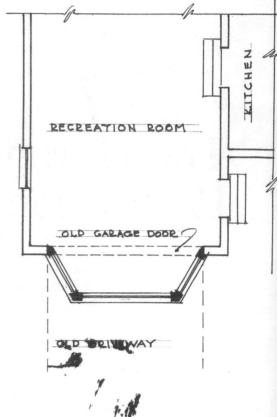

Leveling the Floor

Garage floors are not level. They are sloped from the back to the front so that water from washing the cars or rain that seeps in will run out to the driveway rather than puddling in the garage. In most areas, garages must be several steps down from the floor of the house. This is to prevent a fire in the garage from spreading to the house by burning oil or gasoline running under the door.

You can build up the garage floor, using the back of the garage as the leveling point if there is an exit door there that you want to keep. This can mean that the recreation room will be a step or two down from the floor of the house. You can, instead, use the floor of the house as the leveling point for establishing the floor of

the recreation room. Neither way is right or wrong; which you use will depend on your particular situation.

When putting a new wall over a masonry one, or when leveling a wall to hide pipes and ducts, the 2-by-4s that hold the new wall away from the old one are called furring strips. Essentially, the leveling of a garage floor is the same process, except the lumber used to support the new floor is called sleepers instead of furring strips.

The sleepers are cut to equalize the difference between the back and the front of the garage, and are nailed to the concrete floor using special concrete nails. Shims (pieces of wood shingles) are hammered under the sleepers to insure a perfectly level finished floor.

Plywood, ½ inch thick, is used over the sleepers, placed 16 inches on center as the

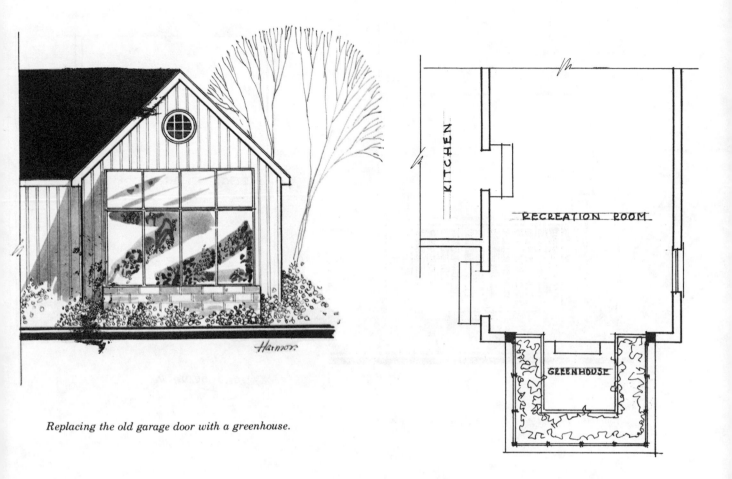

Replacing the old garage door with a greenhouse.

subfloor. If carpet is to be the finished floor, the underpadding can be placed directly on the plywood. If tile is to be used, it is advisable to put down another layer of ¼-inch thick plywood that is called "sanded one side." If hardwood floors are to be used, the subfloor should be covered with a layer of building paper to prevent dampness from the concrete from warping the wood.

If the new floor level is higher than the door sill of a door you want to keep, the door can be raised in its existing location by removing it and lifting the head to the desired height. Studs are almost always doubled on each side of a door. Only one stud on each side, the one closest to the door, has to be removed, along with the construction at the top of the door frame. These studs are then cut to size and replaced.

Blocking Up the Door

The biggest design consideration that will affect the facade of the house is what is done to block up and enclose the wall space where the big overhead garage doors are. This is a grand opportunity for a bay window, a window seat, or even a greenhouse if you have always wanted one.

It could also be a good place to build a fireplace if you do not want a large window facing the driveway and the street. Whether you decide on a window or a fireplace, you will want to remove a section of the driveway from in front of the old garage door location so it does not dissappear under the house. Or, instead of removing a section of the drive, you could use it as a base for a raised planter to soften the facade.

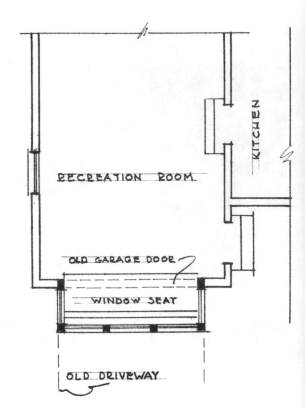

Replacing the old garage door with a window seat.

Do not completely block off the driveway from the new recreation room because it can become an excellent second entrance. A separate entrance will permit family and guests to enter the recreation room directly from the driveway where their cars are parked. There may already be an access to the garage other than the big garage doors, but it probably is not near the driveway. By all means keep the second door — an area as large as a garage should have a second entrance, not only for convenience, but for safety. A second door will also come in handy if you are entertaining in the backyard in the summer, especially if you are including a bathroom in your recreation room plans.

The driveway entrance to the recreation room should be placed in the garage door opening next to the house. This will put it as near to

the kitchen door as possible, and you will not have to cross the width of the room to get to the door. The second door should be at the back of the garage.

Heating and Ventilation

Heat for the recreation room can be brought through the foundation wall of the house. This is made considerably easier by the difference in levels between the house and the garage floors. Even if you use the back of the garage floor to level the new floor instead of building it up to the house floor, there will be space to bring the heating ducts through.

The slope of a garage floor should be a minimum of ¼ inch to the foot, so for a garage 20 feet long there would be a 5-inch difference between the back of the garage and the

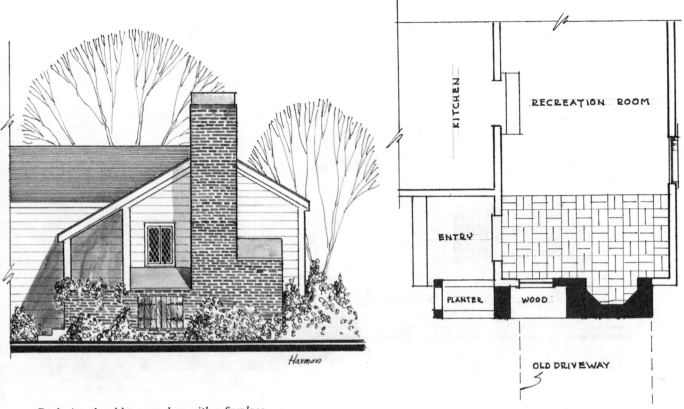

KITCHEN

RECREATION ROOM

ENTRY

PLANTER

WOOD

OLD DRIVEWAY

Replacing the old garage door with a fireplace.

doors — enough space for the heating ducts to be brought through the sleepers to the outside wall. Of course, a separate return duct will have to be included, but that can begin right at the basement or crawl-space wall.

Radiators and hot-water heat present few or no problems because the pipes are small and can be taken through the sleepers to radiators in any location.

If the heating system is already working at maximum capacity, several electric thermostated wall units will keep the chill off in winter. These, combined with a Franklin stove, will provide all the heat you need even on the coldest nights.

For extra ventilation in the summer, build a cupola on the roof. It will create a chimney effect and draw the warm air out of the room. The cupola can be quite small, or large enough

for the children to climb to and use as a crow's nest.

Floors

Because of the wood sleepers and plywood used to level the floor, the floor can be considered the same as new frame construction and any of the finish flooring materials discussed previously can be used. However, because of the existing concrete floor and the sleepers used to level it, there are some interesting alternatives instead of the usual linoleum or tile.

Installing new wood floors that require sanding and finishing in your house is quite a task. Either you have to move all the furniture out of the room, or you must do half the room at a time which means the rented sander will be idle more than half the time as you move furniture, stain, varnish, and wait for it to dry. On

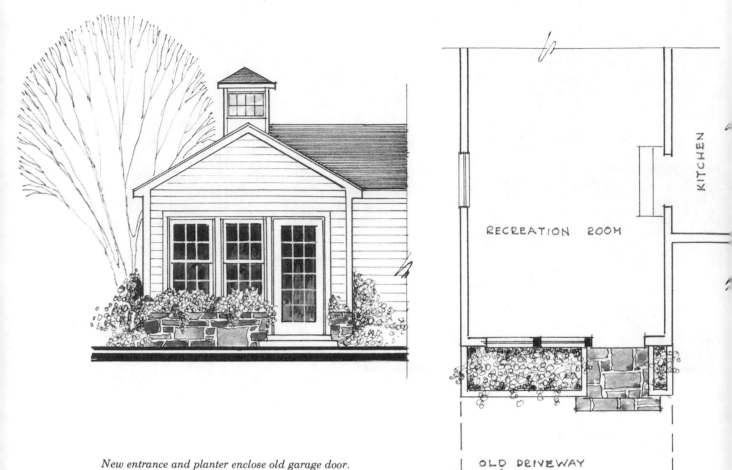

New entrance and planter enclose old garage door.

top of that, no matter how careful you are, fine sawdust will infiltrate the rest of your house and the smell of the stain and varnish will cling to furniture and clothing for several weeks.

You will have none of these problems with a new wood floor in the garage. There is no furniture in the garage and it can be closed off from the rest of the house, so here is the place to install wide plank floors and a slate, flagstone, brick, or ceramic tile entrance if you want. You can also use the concrete floor of the garage as the base for a masonry floor, which is difficult to have in a house because of the weight of the material.

The entire floor of the recreation room can be done in brick, stone, or tile, by leveling the garage floor with concrete and laying the masonry on top of it. This can cause a few prob-

lems with heating ducts and water lines, but the main disadvantage is the cold hard surface of a masonry floor over such a large area.

It is better and much more interesting to keep the masonry at entrances. Wet boots and umbrellas can then be left there to dry without fear the dripping water will do any harm, as it might to a more delicate floor. The floor of an entrance always gets the most abuse and masonry will not wear out.

Walls and Ceilings

The walls can be of any material, but if you want to take advantage of the concrete-floor base of the garage, you can do one wall in brick veneer. Brick on the wall between the recreation room and the house would reduce noise penetration considerably.

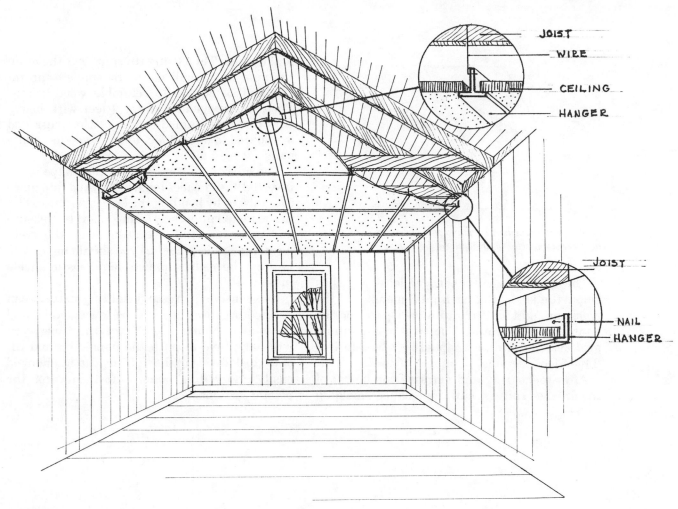

Installation of a hung ceiling in the garage.

Cork or acoustical tile on the wall between the house and recreation room will reduce not only the noise carried through the wall, but the noise level within the room as well. Acoustical tile can either be glued or stapled to furring strips placed against the wall, but it will not take rough use without showing damage.

For an unusual, soft, sound-deadening wall between the house and recreation room, cover the wall with carpet. Carpet can be tacked and stretched into place, just as it is on the floor, and in the long run is not much more expensive than gypsum board that needs taping, spackling, and painting.

The ceilings of many garages are left unfinished and used to store lumber and ladders. A garage does not contain the usual pipes and ducts found in basement ceilings, so it can be a good place to install a hung ceiling.

Installing a Hung Ceiling

A hung, or suspended, ceiling can be installed in one day and can cost less than a new gypsum ceiling. This is especially true if the garage roof is constructed of prefabricated trusses 2 to 4 feet on center, as so many of them are. For a gypsum-board ceiling, you need joists every 16 inches. Putting up the joists and gypsum board, and doing the taping, spackling, and painting takes time and money.

The effect of a suspended ceiling is light and it not only gives you an acoustical ceiling, but inexpensive lighting panels as well. The one big disadvantage of a hung ceiling is its commercial appearance. No matter how tastefully and imaginatively a room is decorated, if it has a suspended ceiling it always reminds me of my dentist's office.

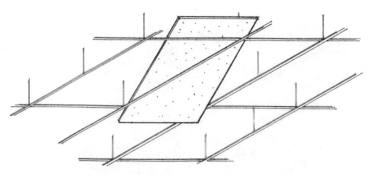

Hung ceiling panels are easily lifted out and can be acoustical material or translucent light panels.

The ceiling is suspended at least 3 inches below the joists, the horizontal member of the truss, or light fixtures to allow space for the panels to be removed. The steel or aluminum grid systems can be adapted to 2-by-2-foot or 2-by-4-foot sections.

After measuring and marking the height of the finished ceiling, nail the L-shaped molding to the walls. Then using tin snips, cut the main runners, which will be in the shape of an inverted T or square to resemble wood beams. These are suspended every 4 feet with heavy wire tied and stapled to the joist or truss and are spaced to hang 4 feet apart if you are using panels 2-by-4 feet.

The cross members, also in the shape of an inverted T and 4 feet long, are locked into place every 2 feet by bending the ends over into a slot in the main runners. It is important to measure and space carefully because after the cross members are in place, all you should have to do is drop the ceiling panels and plastic sheets into place.

Inexpensive fluorescent lighting fixtures can be used because they will be concealed behind the plastic panels. To change the tubes, you will only have to push the panels up and lift out. The location of the lighting can be changed easily and ceiling panels substituted for the plastic sections.

8
Furnishings and Equipment

Furnishing a recreation room can demand all your ingenuity because there are so many conflicts. The older members of the family may want a billiard table and a bar, while the youngsters want a soda fountain. A Ping-Pong table may be constantly appropriated to set up track to run an extensive electric train collection. The room will be wanted for Friday night poker and beer; the Thursday afternoon bridge club and watercress sandwiches; your widowed mother wants it for Wednesday's Senior Citizens Craft Club and tea; your oldest son wants a woodworking shop and his sister needs a place to put the huge loom her grandparents gave her for Christmas.

How you furnish the recreation room will determine how and by whom it will be used. There are bound to be conflicts, but do not make the mistake of trying to please everyone. If you do, you will find that you have satisfied no one and will end up with an expensive and empty room on your hands.

You will have to consider not only the physical space a billiard or Ping-Pong table takes up, but also its spatial prerogatives. People won't enjoy a game of billiards if every time they line up a shot they rap the cue stick into a wall or window. A Ping-Pong game can be seriously disrupted when the score is tied and an overhand blast rips a hole in the sloped ceiling of the attic.

Furniture is as important to a room as seats to an automobile. It determines how many people can use the room, for what purpose, and for how long. You might get to the corner market in a car with a rough box on the floorboards instead of a seat, but it is unlikely that you will make it across the country very quickly or with many passengers for company.

Where there are active games being played, such as Ping-Pong, and there is a change in the floor level, it must always be well marked with a railing. Never, in any room of the house, have a change in level consisting of only one step. Many builders do this so they can advertise a sunken living room or dining room, but people often do not see the one step and fall over it. Even if the difference in levels is, through some quirk in the construction, only 6 inches, make it two 3-inch steps instead of one 6-inch step. The steps should be deep ones, too, at least 10 or 12 inches deep so they will be noticed.

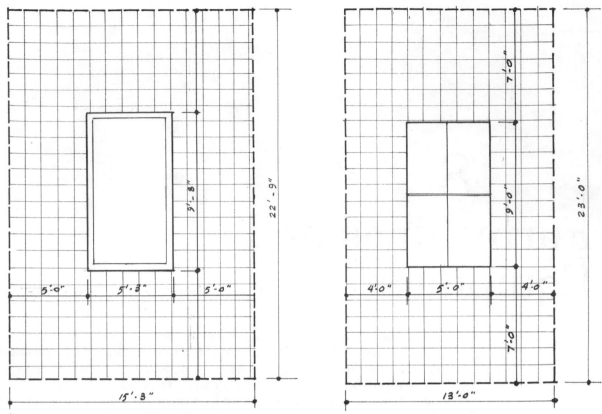

Space requirements for a billiard table (left) and a Ping-Pong table (right).

Billiard or Pool Tables

A standard billiard or pool table is 2 feet 6 inches long. The playing surface is 4 feet 6 inches wide and 9 feet long. However, since the ches wide and 9 feet long. However, since the pool cue and player must have space to maneuver, it is recommended that the long side be 5 feet from a wall and that the short side be 6 feet 6 inches from a wall. Low chairs and tables may encroach on these dimensions, but anything higher than the table, such as a lamp, will get in the way.

Basically, then, you will need a space 15 feet 3 inches wide and 22 feet 9 inches long if you are planning to have a billiard table in the recreation room. The English have a form of billiards called "snooker," the tables for which are larger, measuring 6 feet 9 inches wide and 12 feet 9 inches long, but the clearances at the ends and sides are the same.

The playing surface, conventionally of green felt, should be lighted with a large shaded hanging lamp that will illuminate the entire table without casting shadows. Cues are stored in wall racks nearby. Balls can be left on the table in the rack.

Ping-Pong Table

Table tennis or Ping-Pong is played on a table 2 feet 6 inches high, 5 feet wide, and 9 feet long. There should be a clear space behind each end of the table of at least 7 feet, and there should be 4 feet on each side for the players to swing at the 1-inch balls with the 6-inch-wide and 10½-inch-long bat.

Thus if you are planning a Ping-Pong table for your recreation room, you will need a clear space 13 feet wide and 23 feet long, with a minimum height of 7 feet at all points.

A Ping-Pong table area could be combined with a billiard table area if you allow a width of 15 feet 3 inches (required for billiards) and a length of 23 feet (required for Ping-Pong).

If you are not in training for the Chinese Olympics, a billiard and Ping-Pong table can be combined, although the billiard table, which

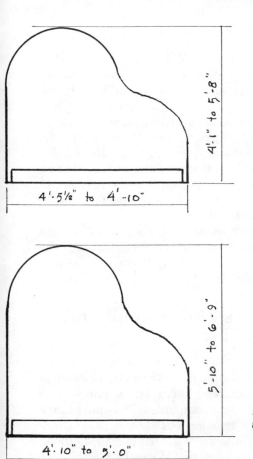

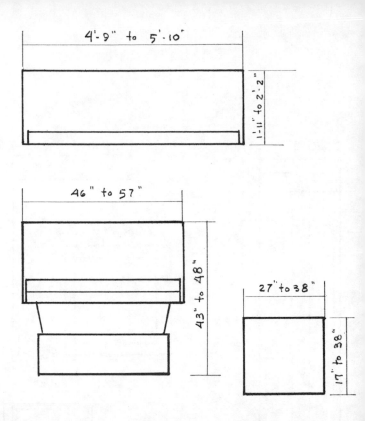

Dimensions of a baby grand piano (top left), living room grand piano (bottom left), upright piano (top, right), and electric organ and speaker box (bottom, right).

will be used as a base, will extend 1½ inches on each side and 4½ inches on each end beyond a standard Ping-Pong table. The lighter Ping-Pong table can be stored folded in half at the net location underneath the billiard table. It can be unfolded on the table and held level with grommets. The lamp, on a scissors extension, can be moved up and out of the way.

Pianos and Organs

There is absolutely nothing like a grand piano to dress up a room, but before you think about moving one into your recreation room, you must consider its weight, size and placement, and make sure that any stairs it is taken up can support its weight and the weight of its carriers.

The long side of a piano, the base section, is always on the left, and since this is the side on which the top is hinged, it is the side that should be placed against the wall. It should also be placed so that the piano player faces the room.

It always looks quite elegant in movies when a piano stands in a handsomely curtained bay window, but in real life, a piano should never be placed in a window where the sun can shine on it. The heat during the day and cool air at night will constantly put the piano out of tune.

Because of the need for a constant temperature, the piano's weight, and the sound factor (which is affected by walls), the best location for a piano is on an inside wall. Piano widths are fairly consistent, between 4 feet 10 inches and 5 feet. Lengths vary from 5 feet 2 inches for a baby grand to 9 feet for a concert grand. The average parlor grand is 6 feet 3 inches long and weighs 700 pounds.

Upright pianos are 4 feet 10 inches long, 2 feet deep, and 3 to 4 feet high. They are available with finished backs and do not have to be placed against a wall. Uprights weigh from 100 to 250 pounds.

Electric organs plug into any grounded convenience outlet. The smallest Hammond spinet is 38 inches high, 45 inches long and 26 inches deep (not counting the seat), and weighs 220

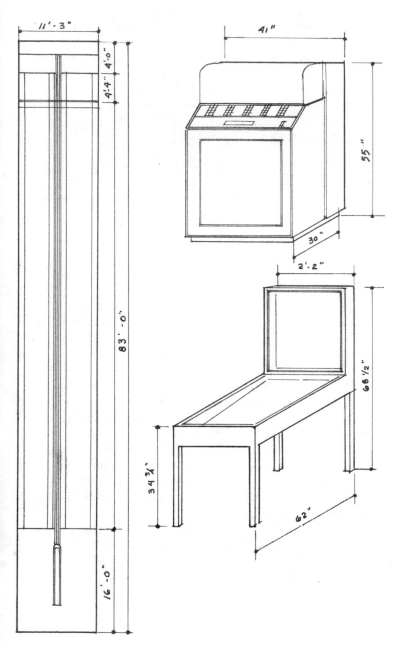

Dimensions of a bowling alley (left), juke box (top right), and pinball machine (bottom right).

pounds. The largest Wurlitzer is 49 inches high, 63 inches long, and 59 inches deep (including floor pedals and seat), and weighs 550 pounds.

It is a good idea to place pianos and organs so that natural light from windows will fall on the performer's left side. Artificial light should also be placed on the left side of the keyboard or on both sides. Try not to place the piano or organ in an isolated corner because people like to gather around and join in. Be sure to consult the dealer from whom you buy the instrument on the proper materials for cleaning the keyboard and for polishing the wood and preserving the finish.

Jukeboxes and Pinball and Slot Machines

Jukeboxes are not as heavy as they look and can be almost any size. You can often buy them secondhand or rent them for a party from music and vending companies. They plug into a standard convenience outlet and can be adjusted so no coins are required to operate them. If you buy the machine, it can be loaded with your own favorite classical or popular records, which you can change (some will hold from 50 to 200 selections).

Pinball machines, which can also be bought or rented from the same music and vending company, plug into a regular convenience outlet. Pinball machines can be adjusted so you can have all the fun of the lights and bells without using coins to operate them.

Pachinco is a Japanese variation of the pinball machine, but it requires no electricity to operate. A Pachinco machine is in itself quite decorative and hangs vertically on the wall. It requires absolutely no skill or intelligence to play. The reward is a series of clanks and bongs as the small metal balls bounce from trap to trap.

Slot machines, sometimes called "one-arm bandits," can also be bought secondhand from various sources, one being the police department in some vicinities where they are illegal in public places and have been confiscated. They may or may not be permitted in private homes, so come to an understanding with local authorities first.

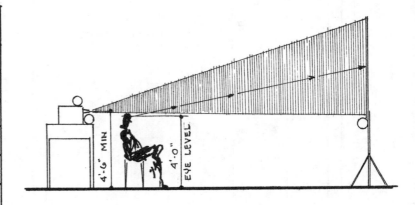

SCREEN SIZE	PROJECTION DISTANCE				
	8 M.M.	16 M.M.			
	1" LENS	1" LENS	1½" LENS	2" LENS	3" LENS
16½"x 22"	11'-0"	5'-0"	7'-6"	10'-0"	..
22"x 30"	14'-6"	6'-9"	10'-0"	13'-6"	..
30"x 40"	19'-6"	9'-0"	13'-6"	18'-0"	26'6"
39"x 52"	25'-0"	11'-6"	17'-0"	23'-0"	34'-6"
45"x 60"	..	13'-0"	19'-6"	26'-6"	40'-0"
54"x 72"	..	16'-0"	24'-0"	32'-0"	48'-0"

Space requirements for film projection.

Slot machines can be adjusted to pay out any percentage of the coins that are fed into them. You can make your guests happy by adjusting it for an enormous number of jackpots, or discourage Junior from gambling and retrieve his exorbitant allowance at the same time by adjusting it to pay out only 1 percent of the take.

Of course, slot machines can be adjusted to operate without using money at all, but this is about as exciting as sitting around a swimming pool with no water in it. If you are afraid guests' feelings will be hurt if they have to dig into their own pockets to play the thing, leave the hinged back unlocked and a cup of coins within reach.

Slot machines are heavy, presumably to prevent people from walking off with them, but their stands can be equipped with rollers so you can roll them away from the wall for cleaning.

Home Movies

Home movies are a pleasant pastime for many families, especially those with growing children. A recreation room where the films can be shown easily, where the projector and screen do not have to be hauled out of closets, and seats arranged only to be laboriously folded and stored after each showing, will considerably increase enjoyment.

Tripod screens are available in sizes from 30-by-40 inches to 72-by-96 inches, but much better and more convenient are wall- or ceiling-mounted screens. These are available in the same sizes as the tripod screens, and up to 6-by-8 feet. They operate just like a window shade (although usually better), and roll into a small box. Many people put them in the valance of a window so that when they are pulled down for showing films or slides, they also keep out exterior light, but they can be placed almost anywhere on a wall or ceiling.

The projector will get more frequent use instead of being reserved for long tiresome periods of time if it has a permanent location in a wall or cabinet opposite the screen. Projectors vary in size, but all are longer than they are wide. If the cabinet space is too small to store the projector so it can be aimed at the screen, the projector can be mounted on a swivel that

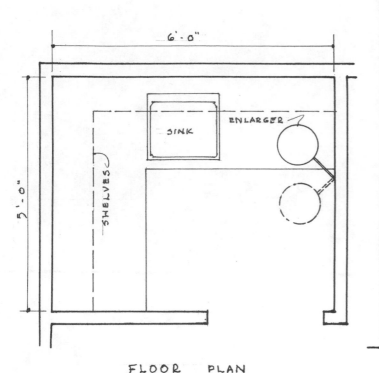

FLOOR   PLAN

WALL   ELEVATION

Plan and elevation of a darkroom.

can be turned sideways as it swings back into the cabinet.

The exact distance the screen should be from the projector depends on the type of film and the lens-focal length of the projector. However, as a rule of thumb, the projector should be at a distance about five and a half times the width of the screen. Therefore, if you have a 40-inch screen, the projector would be about 12 feet away; for a 60-inch screen, about 30 feet away. Individual projectors will be different, and you should check with the dealer before building anything permanently.

Darkrooms

A popular family recreation is photography. A darkroom does not require much space since the only necessary equipment is a cold-water tap and sink, a lightproof door, and several electric outlets. An area 5 by 6 feet is usually adequate.

A 3-foot-high L-shaped counter against two walls will provide space for a sink, film pans, a dryer, a trim board, and a wall-mounted en-

larger. Mount the enlarger so that it can swing over both the counter and the floor, because there may be occasions when you will want to enlarge a tiny detail on a negative into a much larger blowup, and the only way you can get it large enough is by focusing it on paper resting on the floor.

Open shelves over the counter will hold chemicals and other equipment and keep reproduction paper off the counter and within easy reach when you are working with it. At other times, this light-sensitive paper should be stored under the counter, behind doors, and wrapped in its black protective paper.

An additional and vital requirement is ventilation. Use a lightproof louver in the lower half of the door and another high in the wall over the counter. This will allow air to circulate through the door and out through the louver near the ceiling.

You will need one electrical convenience outlet for the enlarger and another for the dryer. You will also need a darkroom light and a regular ceiling light for general work and cleaning. You can have the darkroom light con-

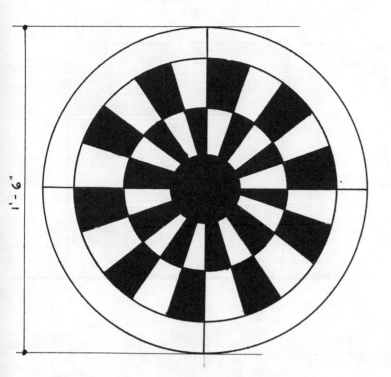

Dart board (left) and chessboard patterns for enlarging.

nected to a warning light on the outside of the door to indicate when the darkroom is in use and the door should not be opened, so that film in process will not inadvertently be ruined.

Dart Boards

Dart boards are fun and you will not find an English pub without one, but they are also dangerous because the 5½-inch darts are heavy and sharp. Dart boards should never be placed on the back of a door into another room or hallway or even close to such a door because someone entering the room quickly or unexpectedly could be seriously hurt.

Darts should be kept away from youngsters. Either store them on a high shelf or leave them in the dart board, which is mounted on the wall at a height of about 5 feet 6 inches. A dart board is 1 foot 6 inches in diameter, and the more or less standard design is painted or printed on cork. Do not use gypsum board as the base for a dart board because it will soon disintegrate.

Tabletop Games and Activities

Chess and checkerboards are interchangeable — a game played on one can be played on the other. Sixty-four 2-inch squares, alternately dark and light, make up a playing area about 16 inches square.

Here, however, the similarity ends. Checkers is a fast game demanding little concentration. It can be played on a steady coffee table in the middle of activity, or on the floor in front of the fireplace. It is especially suited to the fast-paced younger set who can play a quick game or two, using colored stones or bottle caps (Coca-Cola against 7-Up), while sitting on concrete or wooden benches outdoors.

Chess players, on the other hand, require solitude, quiet, and time for contemplation. They want comfortable upholstered chairs to relax in while waiting for opponents to make their moves. Because a friendly game of chess can last for hours or days, and play-by-mail games can take months, a chessboard may require a small table of its own that can be left untouched in an out-of-the-way corner. A chess

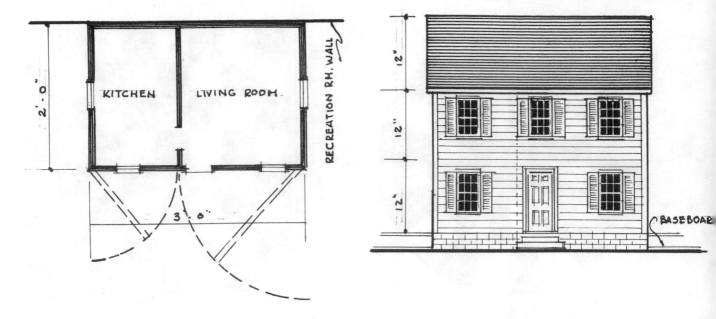

Plan and elevation of a dollhouse for a child's playroom.

table can be easily made by applying a darkening stain every other square in a grid drawn on a small raw wood table before varnishing, and the chessmen can be left in position, always ready for play.

Card tables will serve admirably for most other board games, but jigsaw puzzle enthusiasts may find a use for a working area where they can spread out the pieces right side up and construct the puzzle. Depending on the number of pieces, the puzzle's complexity, and the time available to work on it, a jigsaw puzzle could take months to complete. A good-sized piece of plywood hinged to a wall where it can be drop-leafed out of the way when not in use is convenient, and would be appreciated by all.

Electric Train Sets

Another activity that requires space and, even better, a table of its own is the track setup for electric trains. Sometimes these grow from a circle around the Christmas tree to extensive and valuable collections that include not only the engines and cars, but endless combinations

of track, siding, tunnels, bridges, crossings, stations, water towers, whole villages with trees, landscaping, and street lights.

Electric trains can be a satisfying and enjoyable hobby, and the construction of accessories can occupy many cold wet afternoons that would otherwise be spent thoughtlessly immobile in front of a television set. This hobby also provides a ready gift selection for Christmas and birthdays for years to come.

To be used and enjoyed, a train set must be accessible. The height of a train table will depend on the age of the child, as will the width and whether you can get to it from two or more sides. If the train table is placed against a wall, a depth of 3 feet will be the maximum reach of most six- to ten-year-olds. If the table is accessible from both sides, you can use a 4-by-8-foot sheet of plywood as the surface of the table.

The table will have to be reinforced with 2-by-4s to keep it absolutely rigid and level. If there is any deflection from the weight of trains and accessories, the track can be damaged.

Build the table high enough, at least 30 inches high, so that a toddler with no under-

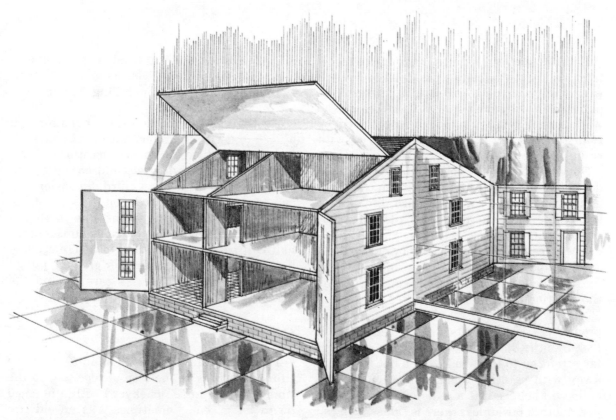

The dollhouse with doors and roof open. Note, mirrors on wall increase and double the illusion.

standing of how the train and transformers operate will not be able to get to the controls or remove the engines and cars from the track.

A 4-by-8-foot table will take up a lot of space, but the train table can be suspended from the ceiling and pulled up and out of the way when not in use. Engines and cars may have to be removed, but these can be stored decoratively on short lengths of track on open shelves.

The hoisting system can be one of pulleys and heavy nylon rope steadied with a clasp fastened to the floor. This system will have to be carefully engineered, and a young child will need the help of an adult to lower the table.

The table could be hoisted to the ceiling using light chain connected to a counterweighted crank. The sides of the train table could be held steady, and slide up and down in a metal track. Regardless of which type is used, a stop should be placed at the top of the system so the miniature buildings, trees, and other accessories do not get crushed against the ceiling.

Most children can operate the counterweighted system easily. The metal side guides are

hinged and held to the floor with grommets. When not in use, they are folded up out of the way against the underside of the train table.

Dollhouses

Little girls, and other miniature fanciers, seem never to tire of dollhouses, and one can be built in the recreation room to be played with and enjoyed now and to serve later as storage. Even after their daughters have given up playing with dolls and are out having cocktails, few mothers can pitch out the ragtag remnants of childhood. Inevitably cloth and thread are taken up to patch the dolls together, and grandchildren are anxiously awaited to pick them up again. What better place to store these dolls than in a dollhouse?

Just how elaborate the dollhouse will be depends on your skill as a craftsman. It will be harder to build, but easier to make look like a real house, if the pieces are cut, painted, and decorated before they are nailed together. Painting and decorating should be as authentic as possible.

Details, such as siding, door and window trim, and shutters, can be painted on after the walls are given a flat coat and a finish coat of paint. If this is done while the sections can be worked on in a flat position, the results will be realistic and you will not be bothered with running paint.

Small inaccessible spaces in the finished dollhouse will be easy to get to if you can paint and paper them on a workbench, but almost impossible when the house is nailed together. And remember, close scrutiny will be given every corner by the young new owner.

Wallpaper, curtains, pictures, and tiny light fixtures made from old earrings can be glued on the interior walls. Carpet samples or pieces of cloth can be glued or tacked to the floors. Appropriate wallpaper glued and varnished will look like tile on the kitchen floor. Pay particular attention to the windows; do not try to get away with painting them on the outside. No child will believe it is a real dollhouse and not just another box unless there is "glass" you can see through in the windows.

Cut holes for the windows and interior doors. The front door can be painted on the exterior and interior. Cut tough clear plastic slightly larger than the window openings and glue matchsticks or thin pieces of balsa wood to it to simulate the window muntins. Glue the plastic over the window opening with the muntins facing the outside.

Pieces of wood shingles can be tacked to the roof, or you can use asphalt shingles cut to scale. If you have no old shingles around, cut rough sandpaper to scale and glue it to the roof to imitate shingles.

Since this dollhouse is being built against the wall of the recreation room, begin by building the base up to a height of the baseboard trim and paint it to resemble the brick or stone foundation of a house. The roof should be hinged several inches in front of the dollhouse ridge so that, when it is open, it will lean against the wall without falling forward and hitting small heads.

The front wall is divided at the partition and hinged to get to the rooms inside. Use a small round cabinet knob in the location of the painted door. This will give children the feeling of opening a real door. A third dimension can be added by gluing mirrors on the wall of the recreation room, tight against the dollhouse walls and as far up as the ridge so the other half will be a reflection and look like a gable house. If you put pots of ivy or growing plants recommended for children's care around the base, it will look like foundation planting.

Swings

The first thing that comes to mind when we think of swings is one loop of rope tied to the limb of a tree in the backyard with a notched board for a seat. Sometimes it is an old tire roped to the tree instead.

However, there are other types, and swings have become popular and fashionable as furniture. There is still the simple child's swing, but it is not used inside because there is too little space and too much furniture to run into.

More sophisticated upholstered swings can be used in a recreation room as nowhere else. They come in all shapes and sizes, from swinging love seats to large wicker cages that have bracket holders for iced drinks, plants, and books.

These swings are not meant to swing in a wide arc, but their gentle motion can be quite pleasant and relaxing. Since there are no legs to vacuum and clean around, they make cleaning quicker and easier. Attach them securely to the ceiling, making sure they are anchored to a joist and the ceiling structure.

9
Special Attractions

A recreation room can have many special features built into it that will increase its value to the home and to the family living there. A fireplace, for instance, can take the heat load off a house heating system that is already working at full capacity before the recreation room is added. An exercise room or gym, complete with sauna or steam bath, can get a family working out together and be enormously beneficial to their physical appearance and their health.

For more sedentary families, a greenhouse can offer instructive recreation and fresh vegetables all year. A greenhouse does not have to be a muddy and functional plant laboratory. It can be an exciting glass cage with a summer terrace atmosphere, and if it is off the kitchen, it can be used for dining, with the glass walls softened by hanging plants and, if height permits, trees bearing fruit and blossoms. This type of room was known in our grandparents' day as an "orangery," and was very valuable in a time before superhighways and refrigerated trucks made fresh Florida fruit commonplace in winter. The old-fashioned orangery was often off the dining room, several stories high, and served as a marvelous breakfast room — an excellent place to begin the day before facing a bleak January morning.

Sauna Baths

Not too many families in the United States are into communal bathing, but the Japanese, Finns, Romans, and Greeks have all used the bath as a source of relaxation, recreation, and communication for centuries. Most ancient bathing took place in bathhouses, which some times reached palatial proportions capable of accommodating 6,000 people at one time, as in Diocletian's thermal baths.

The Japanese use water heated to a temperature of 105° to 115° F. "Sauna" is a Finnish word, and the Finns developed a system of bathing with dry heat that became a family tradition. The customary Finnish sauna is a small log house in which a wood fire heats rocks placed on top of the stove until the air in the room reaches a temperature of 175° F. (for beginners) to 212° F. or more (for

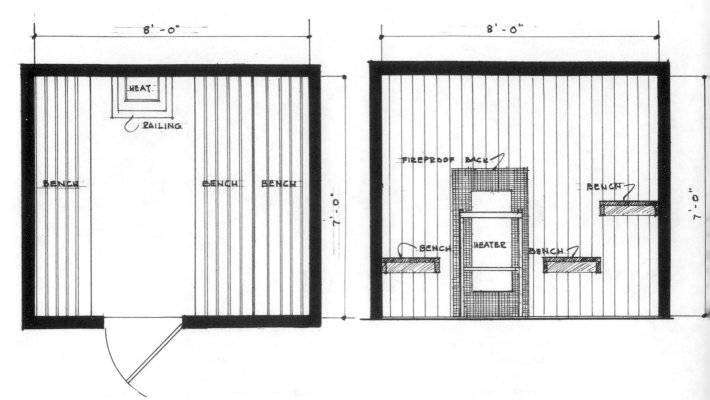

Plan and wall elevation of sauna bath.

experienced sauna bathers). The dryer the air, the hotter the temperature that can be endured. Along with their sauna, the Finns flog themselves with light birch whisks, which loosens the dirt and dried perspiration on the skin and, even more importantly, stimulates blood circulation.

It is also their custom to rush from the sauna to roll naked in snow banks and jump into frozen lakes. It is safe to say this part of the procedure will be omitted by most Americans, although a leisurely plunge into a swimming pool or a cool shower several times during the sauna can be most refreshing.

The psychological effect of a sauna is tranquilizing to the whole nervous system; tensions disappear. Physically, the sauna opens all the pores of the skin and the bather sweats profusely, flushing out of the skin impurities that can never be reached with hot water and soap. This deep cleansing is similar to the difference between sweeping a carpet with a broom and cleaning it with a strong vacuum cleaner.

The full range of health benefits of the sauna has not been fully investigated, but many sauna users experience fewer colds, a marked loss of nervous tension, better sleep, more attractive skin with fewer blemishes, faster-growing hair and fingernails, and, of course, a quick loss of weight because excess water is squeezed out of fatty tissue. You can lose 1 to 3 pounds per bath. This weight will not stay lost unless you limit the amount of liquids you drink for two hours after the sauna. Few endow the sauna with the religious significance the Finns do, but athletes engaged in strenuous sports such as football, downhill skiing, weight lifting, and long-distance running find the sauna essential for maintaining their physical condition.

Although a sauna will relieve the symptoms of a hangover, alcohol should not be taken directly before or after a sauna. Too, sauna baths are not for everyone. If you have a respiratory disorder, heart trouble, or blood pressure problems, consult your doctor before entering a sauna.

Family sauna baths? Of course, unless you are so puritanical or unattractive that you are embarrassed to be seen without your shield of

Interior of sauna.

protective covering. Bathing suits should not be worn in the sauna. They restrict circulation and metal zippers or buckles can get hot enough to burn your skin.

The two technical disadvantages of a sauna are the danger of fire from improper installation and the cost of heating the electric sauna stove. Although the sauna stove is no more complicated or dangerous than an electric range, because of the wood involved in most construction, human error and carelessness, and electrical malfunctioning, things can go wrong. Because of this some insurance companies require separate coverage for saunas. You can ask your utility company the cost of operating a sauna stove.

The size of the sauna will depend on how many people will be using it at the same time. The stay varies from 5 to 15 minutes to over an hour and a half. There should be enough space on the benches to recline so that the temperature is even all over your body. Usually the room is 5 to 7 feet wide, 6 to 8 feet long, and 7 feet high — large enough to accommodate six people.

The floor, walls, ceiling, and door must be insulated and have an aluminum foil vapor barrier facing the room. If the existing joists and studs are uncovered, they should be covered with ½-inch gypsum board, and new studs installed to hold the insulation.

Usually there are no windows in the sauna, but if you want one, use insulating glass. There should be a small window in the sauna door, which always swings out. There should never be a lock on the door and it should be equipped with a pneumatic door closer. Since any metal gets very hot, the door should be built to push open from inside the sauna and it should have no exposed hardware on it.

The floor can be tile or concrete sloped to a drain. Do not use indoor-outdoor carpet because it will absorb perspiration and become rather pungent in time. The same is true of wood or wooden duckboards, with the added disadvantage that these become slippery when wet.

The walls and ceiling are usually covered with unfinished kiln-dried tongue-and-groove redwood or cedar. The area around the stove

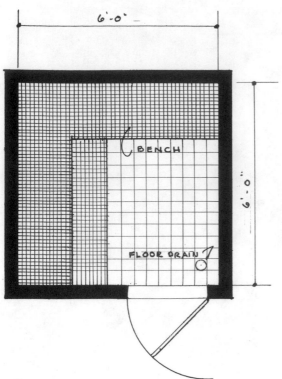
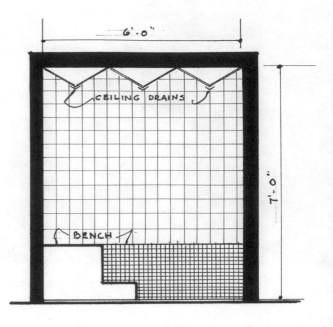

Plan and elevation of steam bath.

must be lined with asbestos cement wallboard such as Transite.

The benches can be built of redwood, but because this wood can stain and irritate sensitive skin, most people prefer white pine. Nails are hot-dipped galvanized and must be countersunk so there is no possibility of getting burned by sitting on a hot nail head.

The 20-inch-wide benches are built in tiers, the first tier 18 inches above the floor and the top one no closer than 42 inches to the ceiling. The temperature in the sauna will increase 12° F. for every foot in height.

Lighting is done by a vaporproof insulated light recessed into the ceiling, controlled by a switch outside the sauna door. The switch should not be in the room.

Ventilation must be provided by vents in the wall at the floor and ceiling. Their size is figured at 10 square inches for every 100 cubic feet of sauna. One vent is placed near the stove 12 inches from the ceiling, and another on an adjacent wall 12 inches from the floor.

There are a number of sauna stoves that are heated by electricity, with the heat-retaining stones on the top. They should have a wooden railing built around them to keep people from stumbling against them. Some people can become dizzy, either from the unaccustomed heat of the sauna or from lack of air due to overcrowding.

The sauna can be bought in a prefabricated unit, but since these must be shipped from a factory, it is usually no more expensive to have one custom built. The heater for a 6-by-8-foot sauna (one large enough for five or six people) is a 7½-kilowatt (7,500 watts, about the same as for a kitchen range) stove that requires a separate 240-volt electric line.

The cost will vary a bit with the size, but basically the equipment is the same. Prices for a custom-built 6-by-8-foot sauna in 1976 were between $1,900 and $3,800, depending on the location and the existing structure.

In addition to the sauna itself, you will want a shower and a small room to relax in between sessions. If this can be at poolside, so much the better. Even so, because you will be perspiring heavily, you should shower before you go into the pool. The room should be comfortable, as

The tile interior of a steam bath with channels to drain condensation off the ceiling.

this relaxation period between saunas is an important aspect in obtaining the maximum benefits. With such a room, twice the number of people will be able to use the sauna because while half are in the sauna, the other half can be showering and relaxing.

Steam Baths

Steam baths, steam rooms, steam cabinets, and Turkish baths are all the same thing, and are not at all like a sauna, although they can be just as beneficial. Steam cleans and stimulates the skin, relaxes muscles, eases tension, and soothes nerves — and since it is inhaled, it can be beneficial to lungs and bronchial tubes.

A sauna is very dry; a steam bath is wet. Although the temperature of the air in a steam bath is much lower (a maximum of 150° F., which is more than most people can tolerate), a steam room seems much hotter than a sauna. Because of the water-laden air and the constant condensation on the walls, floor, and ceiling, the construction of a steam room is similar to that of a sauna, but the finishing materials must be different.

The walls, ceiling, and floor must be insulated and the floor must have a drain to handle the condensation and for cleaning. Wood and metal should be avoided because wood will rot and metal can get too hot. The best wall-finishing material is ceramic tile. The floor can be concrete or slip-proof tile.

Because the steam will condense on the ceiling, it can drip on the bathers and make them uncomfortable. This can be avoided if the ceiling slopes in a series of short panels that drip the condensation into small gutters. These, in turn, can deposit the water into a wall drain or simply empty it on the floor so it can be carried off by the floor drain.

Benches need to be in only one tier and must be waterproof. Wood will rot, swell, and splinter. Concrete is best for the benches because it can be tiled with ceramic like the walls.

A vaporproof light fixture must be used and the switch should be outside the steam room. The door should be insulated and waterproof, with no lock, and open out from the steam room. It should have a window in it so you do not open it in someone's face.

A Franklin stove installed in a relaxing get-together recreation room.

Fireplaces and Franklin Stoves

Building a fireplace is not a do-it-yourself project. Even most experienced masons find it difficult if not impossible to build a fireplace that does not smoke. A Franklin stove, which is preengineered, is a much better project to tackle yourself.

The consideration for the placement of a Franklin stove and a masonry fireplace are the same. Neither should be placed near windows. The heat from the stove or the stovepipe can crack the glass, and either can ignite curtains if they are hung too close. Doors, either to other rooms or to the exterior, should be as far away as possible from the fireplace so that it is not in a circulation area and so furniture can be placed around it.

Franklin stoves must be set forward in the room away from the wall unless the wall is of masonry. Even then, air must be allowed to circulate around and behind the stove. The manufacturer's installation instructions should be followed to the letter. A Franklin stove will produce more heat, faster and more economically, than any masonry fireplace.

The Franklin stove requires no foundation and no masonry chimney. The flue is metal stovepipe on the interior of the house and is taken through the roof with an insulated stainless-steel sleeve. The lightweight prefabricated chimney section is supported by the roof. A damper, if desired, can be placed in the stovepipe just above the top of the stove.

Instead of a masonry wall or masonry veneer behind the stove, you could use a sheet of asbestos concrete. This will speed up the installation of the stove, which can then be accomplished in one day. The only disadvantage of a Franklin stove is that the ashes must be removed and carried out of the house by hand. This can be dusty work, and ashes can get sprinkled around the room.

If you prefer a masonry fireplace, design it to be built on a raised hearth with an ash drop in the foundation and a metal trapdoor in the floor of the fireplace (located under the flue position). This will allow you to drop ashes into the foundation through the door, and than remove

A recreation room combined with a conventional greenhouse.

the ashes from the outside of the house, even if the floor level of the room is only inches from the ground.

Greenhouses

The location of a greenhouse will depend on the orientation of your home. South is the best location, southeast is the second choice. West is too shaded most of the day and too hot when it does get sun in summer. You can grow a limited number of green shade plants in a greenhouse on the northern side of the house, but not the vegetables and the many flowering plants and trees that you can grow in a greenhouse on the southern side of the house.

The recreational greenhouse is probably best placed off the kitchen where it is close to water lines and the food preparation area and distant from the quiet bedroom area. Also, youngsters can be supervised easily here. A recreational greenhouse could, however, be placed off a living room or dining room if there is access from the kitchen for serving, arranging flowers, and washing vegetables.

Commercial greenhouses are always exciting places and the same concept can be used for a recreational greenhouse. If it is to be room-sized, a separate heating system and thermostat will have to be included.

If large orange trees, grapefruit, lemon, or lime trees are to be planted, the soil under the greenhouse will have to be vermin-proofed because large trees cannot survive in pots or tubs. Large fruit-bearing trees are one of the joys of a greenhouse, but need a ceiling height of at least 12 feet.

Small bushes, flowers, vegetables, grapes, and vines for shade will grow in deep pots or in planting benches. Cherry tomatoes, peppers, cucumbers, herbs, and many other small plants can be grown in decorative hanging containers.

The floor of the greenhouse will be a base of concrete with whatever finish is desired, except in those areas where large trees are to be placed. Raised planting benches combined with hanging containers can provide enough growing space for flowers and vegetables.

The main planting beds are the two- or three-tiered wooden benches. The planting

A modern interpretation of a combined greenhouse and recreation room with a swimming pool, off the kitchen and living room of a contemporary house.

area is lined with metal or plastic and drained so that occasional overwatering will not harm the plants. The tiers will assure that the plants get adequate sunshine and permit the separation of plants requiring different amounts of moisture and fertilizer.

Watering can be done with a hose or by a built-in system. The latter comes in several types, one being completely automatic and working off a timer and humidistat similar to the automatic thermostat that controls your furnace. The amount of automation varies. Another, more basic type has built-in pipes, but the water is controlled by a hand valve.

Water connections can be managed with as much simplicity as a hose or plastic pipe that only has to be glued together. Plastic pipe can be used for both the supply and drain, and since it can be sawed and glued together easily, changes can be made to accommodate different arrangements.

A fountain and pool can be included. All that is necessary is an electrical connection to power the small pump. The pool and fountain will create additional moisture in the greenhouse, which is good for the plants, but on hot summer nights it will also increase the humidity in the air, which is uncomfortable for people. A fountain will block out outside sounds and traffic noise, helping to create an atmosphere of peaceful relaxation and detachment.

A dehumidifier connected to a drain can help relieve the dampness. Usually the high ceiling of the greenhouse and adequate ventilation is enough to keep both plants and people comfortable on the hottest summer nights.

Since heat rises, the high ceiling itself will help the room cool. The heat can be let out by opening screened vents at the ridge. These are operated by turning a worm gear placed within easy reach. Small electric fans in the gable ends of the roof will also draw off warm air that has risen to the ridge and keep circulation moving.

The plants themselves can help shade the greenhouse. If there is space, you can include a grape arbor, which will shade part of the greenhouse in summer. Grape vines, like all deciduous plants, lose their leaves in the fall,

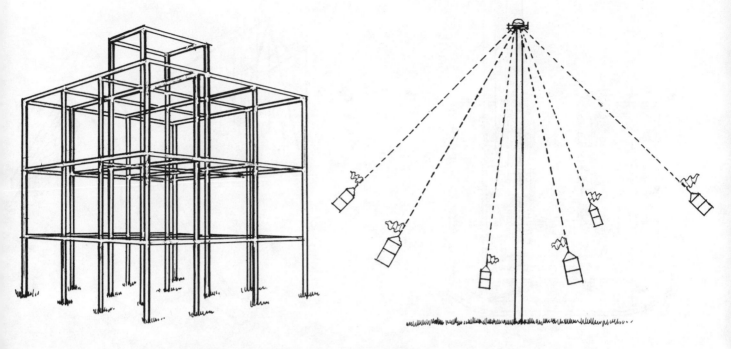

Playtime equipment includes (left) a jungle gym for climbing and (right) a giant stride merry-go-round.

so the warming sun will filter through in the winter. The grape arbor could be placed on the outside of the greenhouse for about the same effect. Grape vines will also grow on a trellis if it is strong enough to support them.

Other annual plants in the form of vines can be grown on trellises, rope, or even string to shade the greenhouse in the summer. Good choices are morning glories or moonvine, which blooms at night. Ivy needs no support and will grow on anything. However, it usually does so well in a greenhouse that it needs to be trimmed back in the fall to permit sunlight to penetrate during the winter.

Greenhouses and fireplace are not mutually exclusive, and the latter can provide pleasant heat on cold evenings. Other methods of heating the greenhouse are heat lamps and radiant heat in the concrete floor.

Heat lamps are installed just as any other lighting and provide heat as well as light. Many commercial greenhouses use these to simulate sunlight and advance the blooms of plants so that lilies, for instance, burst into bloom by Easter Sunday.

Since the floor is concrete, you can also have radiant heat pipes imbedded in it when the concrete is being poured. Installation of pipe is expensive, but operation is economical.

Children's Play Areas

Children need very little structure in their play areas, and most are just as happy with packing boxes and mud as they are with a lot of expensive recreational contrivances. Several pieces of standard equipment will attract them to the area, though, such as the seesaws, swings, and sandboxes traditional to children's playgrounds. Usually thought of as outdoor equipment, all of these, and the following, can be built for indoor use, too.

Certain precautions should be taken to make the area as safe as possible. Concrete is easy to keep clean, but it is hard and can injure knees and elbows. Grass stains clothing, but will not do the damage to young limbs that harder surfaces will. Play equipment on grass should be rotated periodically to keep the grass growing and alive.

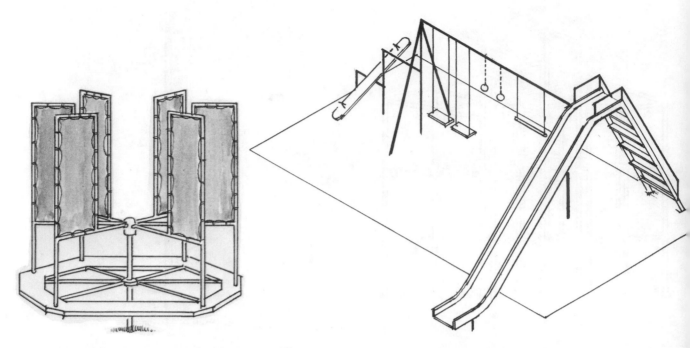

A merry-go-round with canvas sails (left) and a seesaw, swings and slide arrangement are also possibilities for a children's play area.

Indoor-outdoor carpet can also be used, but when used outdoors over concrete, it is a very hard surface. If you do use it outdoors, do not vacuum it when it is wet or damp. You could get a nasty shock through an improperly grounded vacuum cleaner.

Indoor seesaws should be carefully sized so they cannot rise high enough to hit heads against the ceiling. Some adults cannot resist seesaws, and this should be taken into account when calculating headroom and the size of the board. A seesaw should be placed well away from windows so a child cannot fall against the glass if he tumbles off.

Swings should also be strong enough to support an adult, and should never be placed near a window or swing toward one. Children are never content to swing gently back and forth and will twist and turn the swing in all directions. There are swing sets commercially available if you do not have a big tree with a sturdy limb in your backyard. If the swing is to be placed inside the house, do not assume that you can use an existing joist for the support. Add a new double joist to support the swing.

Sandboxes should be built off the ground so air can circulate under them on a base of waterproof plywood. Fill them only with sterilized sand, which should be replaced every year. Indoors or out, they should be fenced to keep pets and stray animals away since children can be infected with their droppings.

A jungle gym can be built using steel pipe and standard connections. Stainless steel is the most attractive and never needs painting. It should be placed over grass, sand, or some soft surface so that tots who take a fall will not be seriously injured. If you think this is going to be a problem, make a wider metal ring around the bottom of the outside 2 feet above ground and suspend canvas or a net secured to steel springs to cushion any falls from the top or sides. You can also suspend some gymnasium rings and a swing from the horizontal top members of the gym.

Children of any age like slides and these should be strong enough to support several adults, too. The slide should always be a continuous piece of stainless steel or smooth plastic. Guards should be installed on the ladder

A tee, driving net, and putting rug for the golfer who wants to practice his game in the winter.

and at the top of the slide to prevent tumbles.

A merry-go-round will also intrigue children. Built on a universal joint with ball bearings, it will need no power except the action of children pushing it around as they jump on. If it is to be outdoors, attractive canvas sails that catch the wind can turn it.

A shallow pool for wading and for sailing boats can be built out of concrete and concrete block. Since it is only one block deep, there is not a great deal of water pressure or the construction problems retaining the soil. Several coats of swimming-pool paint on top of a silicone waterproofing base will be enough to hold the water. It can be filled from the hose, although it should be equipped with a drain to a dry well for cleaning. If outdoors, it can be used, half-filled, for ice skating in the winter.

A playhouse can be built either indoors or out, but if it is outside, you should build it as if it were a garden house or any other permanent structure. It does not require a concrete foundation and foundation walls; it can be built on posts set into the ground. It should be structurally sound, and since boys are bound to use it as

a clubhouse, it should be able to be locked but from the outside only. Walls are constructed of 2-by-4-inch studs and finished on the outside with exterior plywood. The doors and windows should be real, but shutters, clapboard, brick or stone, and details can be painted on.

Indoor Golf

You do not have to let your golf swing get rusty during the winter. To find out what you can do indoors to improve your golf game, I consulted Robert Frank Lewis, an architect who teaches golf in Lake Worth, Florida, and Southampton, New York.

One of the best and least expensive ways of improving your golf game indoors is with the use of a net. The net, 8 feet high and 12 feet wide, can be hung from a drapery track fastened to the ceiling. The track will allow you to push it out of the way when it is not in use. Though the net is of heavy nylon, it is light in weight (about 4½ pounds). Nylon will not throw a portion of the room into darkness when it is drawn across the room for practice as canvas would. For safety's sake, it should not be hung directly in front of windows.

Canvas can be used instead and some golfers prefer it because of the resounding smack it makes when hit. However, canvas is very heavy, requires bulkier support, and when drawn for practice, it can cut off needed light. Twelve feet of it also tends to create an unattractive mass when pushed against the wall. Net will fold inconspicuously away and not be noticed. The net, of course, is easily moved outdoors in the summer.

A mat of a nonslip rubber base, topped with synthetic fiber resembling turf and similar to those used at driving ranges, is used to hit from. The mat will have holes for rubber tees, but you can also use a hemp or cocoa doormat for hitting. There are also instructional mats for beginners that show the position of feet, ball, clubhead, hands, and swing of the club.

The mat can be placed as close to the net as your swing will permit, but usually a distance of 9 to 12 feet is preferred. The mat is used as a base for hitting the ball into the net, which catches the ball and lets it slip gently to the floor.

The largest driver is 3 feet 8 inches long, and the highest point the clubhead reaches, or should reach, on a 6-foot golfer is about 8 feet 2 inches. This means that a golfer of average height can be seriously inhibited by the usual 8-foot ceiling on a drive with a full swing. Even if he does not actually hit the ceiling, the possibility that he might is intimidating, especially if he knows that if he does hit the ceiling, so

will his wife. A ceiling height of 10 feet is recommended.

The net is not only good for exercise, it also offers a unique advantage in practicing. Instead of concerning yourself with *where* the ball is going, you can concentrate on *how* it should be hit. The more you practice properly, the stronger and straighter you will become.

A full-length mirror is a great help in checking your stance. With it, you can correct your grip, elbow position, hunching, any sway, and your position at the top of the backswing. Films taken of your swing can also indicate faults that need to be corrected. Also, plastic balls, aimed directly at the mirror, will drop off without damage and let you analyze your follow-through.

Golf aids for your swing abound, from straps to cure "flying elbows" to a metal contrivance that falls apart if it detects a flaw. There is also a golf ball attached to a swivel and one attached to a cord fastened to a calibrated shaft that measures a drive up to 250 yards, indicating the flight of the ball.

To help you with putting practice, there are floor cups that rest on top of the carpet. The carpet will not be the same as a green, but it can substitute for your favorite pastime while watching the news. You can also get an electric cup that automatically returns successful putts you at the distance you have set it for. These are also available operated on battery power. Others do not require power and eject the ball using a balanced and counterweighted spring system.

10
Outdoor Areas and Activities

Outdoor recreation rooms can be in all shapes and sizes and they need not be spaces enclosed as rooms. An outdoor recreation room can be a separate structure, such as a pavilion or a detached greenhouse used for growing plants and relaxing in the sun winter and summer. It can be a poolside cabana used for changing clothes, relaxation between swimming, and sauna bathing. The recreation room can be a semipermanent tent raised for a weekend or a vacation season or for special entertaining.

The recreation space can be an arbor used to shade each end of a shuffleboard court and for a glass of iced tea between games. Or, it could be a roofless area defined by high hedges to enclose a croquet lawn, back up a badminton court, and keep the wind off players.

For the golfer, the outdoor recreation room could be an open-sided shed facing a net so that on rainy Saturday mornings and Sunday afternoons, he can practice his drives and chip shots. It will be cheaper than renting all those buckets of balls at the driving range. You can include a putting green and a sand trap. Grass greens require an enormous amount of upkeep; indoor-outdoor carpet can be used as a substitute. The carpet will have to be placed on concrete or some other firm waterproof base. Carpet over grass will rot the grass and it will smell and become a haven for insects. Placed over sand, carpet will not be firm and will leave impressions of your shoes, which will drive you mad when you try to putt.

Some games, such as badminton, require only a certain amount of flat area and a net. Others, such as tennis, require a court that involves real construction, whether it be made of grass, clay, or composition. It must be fenced or have backdrops at least 10 feet high, plus strong net supports. If there is to be no permanent structure, you probably will not have to apply for a building permit, although in some cases a building permit is required for the construction of just a tennis court.

One advantage of using a tent for recreation is that it usually does not require a building permit. A huge one erected on your lawn for a wedding and reception involving many people may require a permit on a temporary basis, but this is usually only to alert the police to unusual traffic and parking.

A golf pavilion for practicing drives and a putting green. The doors of the pavilion slide open like old-fashioned barn doors and are held firmly in place on tracks supported by girders.

Pavilions

A pavilion can be a small, simple, and playful structure built on piers with lightweight walls made of lath or canvas, suspended from heavier columns and beams. It can be nothing more than a detached outdoor porch, or it can be as structurally complicated as a home itself, with bathrooms and cooking facilities, heat and air conditioning.

It can be a prefabricated metal-and-wood structure, but usually this is poorly designed and requires all the permits and observations of the building code demanded for conventional constructions. And a prefabricated structure will not improve your property value to the extent that a traditionally built structure will, if it has true design quality.

The location of a pavilion should be carefully chosen so it ends up doing more than just providing space for recreation. It should screen unwanted views, block noise from the street, become part of the garden setting, and enhance the view of the garden from the main windows of the house. Drainage and a set-back regula-

tions should also be investigated since so-called outbuildings may not be permitted in your neighborhood.

The structure should be similar to that of the house in design, materials, and color, but it need not be a slavish copy of a Colonial, Spanish, or other design. Since it will be used a great deal in the summer months, wide overhangs will protect the interior from the sun and rain. An overhang of 4 feet is usually generous enough to permit doors and windows to be left open so you can enjoy watching the rain.

Water, in the form of a simple hose bib, or more complicated plumbing, in the form of a sink or a bathroom, should be run to a pavilion, not only for cleaning purposes, but also as a handy protection in case of fire. A water connection for summertime use can be made from the basement of your house and run in plastic pipe to the pavilion. However, this would only be to a hose bib, which will have to be turned off during the winter. For a year-round system, regular pipes, vents, and drains will have to be

A relax-in-comfort pavilion cantilevered over the swimming pool, surrounded by a high garden wall.

installed, along with heat to keep the system from freezing in the winter.

Heating a pavilion to take the chill off in spring and fall can be done with a fireplace, Franklin stove, electric heater, or a regular furnace. If electric heat is to be used during the winter months, heavy insulation will be required to conserve fuel. Small oil-fired furnaces using forced warm air, similar but smaller than those in homes, can be installed to heat a pavilion. To avoid masonry, erect a prefabricated lightweight chimney.

If heat, light, and plumbing, or any of the three, are to be brought to the pavilion, the same strict regulations regarding health, safety, and fire prevention that apply to house construction must be followed.

You will need to conform to zoning ordinances and building codes. A set of plans will have to be submitted to the building department to obtain a building permit. In determining the cost, you must remember that filing with the building department automatically requires a reexamination of the value of your property and an inevitable increase in property taxes. This is equally true of both pavilions and cabanas, so investigate the added cost in taxes before beginning construction.

Cabanas

A cabana is always located beside a pool or beach and is used to change clothes for swimming. The main difference between a cabana and a pavilion is that a cabana will have a bathroom and perhaps some cooking facilities since it is also used for entertaining. A shower is a necessity before entering the pool and before getting dressed. This will be especially true if you incorporate a sauna or steam room into the cabana. Then the usual social area separating the men's dressing room from the women's can become a relaxation room between sauna baths.

Electricity in a cabana and into a pool area should always be handled very carefully to avoid the danger of shock. Water should be kept off the floor as much as possible. Mercury switches are slightly safer because they only need to be touched to turn them on and off.

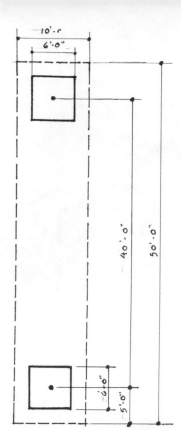 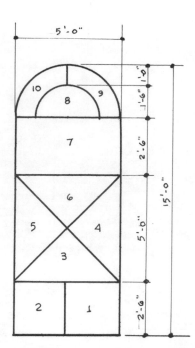 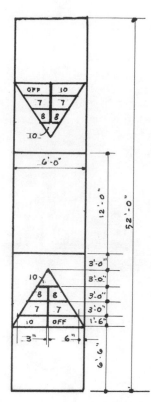

Layout for horseshoes (left), one of the oldest American games still in existence, hopscotch (center), the perennial favorite of children on city sidewalks or backyard, and Shuffleboard (right), recreation for adults from Florida to ships at sea.

Heating is not too much of a problem in a cabana unless you use it for a sauna in the winter. Never use portable electric heaters in a cabana; there is too much danger of shock. If the pool and cabana are closed down in winter, you need no heat. Otherwise use a conventional heating system of forced warm air or radiant heat.

Tents

A delightful, if temporary, recreation room can be created with a tent. It is supported on a pipe structure and can be taken down and stored when not in use.

The most important considerations are that the tent is well anchored so it will not collapse in the wind, and that it is not constructed of inflammable plastic or other material that will burn. Never use a plastic or plastic-coated material that will give off toxic fumes or melt and drip down in flaming globs.

The floor can be grass if it is in good condition or concrete if the tent is to be reused year after year. You can also use wooden duck boards made into squares so that they can be taken up and stored for the winter.

Lighting with kerosene lanterns and torches will present the danger of fire. Temporary electric wiring can also be dangerous, especially if the wires are touching the metal tent supports because this can cause short circuits in wet weather. Battery-powered lamps can be used safely, as can covered hurricane lamps if they are kept on sturdy tables in the center and not along the outside walls.

Plastic Bubbles

These have been used as covers for swimming pools in Seattle and tennis courts at Forest Hills. Bubbles can be used all year except in areas with exceptionally high winds. They must have a substantial base, such as concrete.

A plastic bubble has no structural support. It is nothing more than a big balloon inflated with air and kept that way under light pressure from one or more pumps. To keep the bubble from sagging every time a door is opened, entrance must be through an air lock to equalize the pressure. There should be a door at each end.

The base of the bubble is held in place in a number of ways, depending on the manufacturer and the building code in effect in your area (which will specify the wind bracing and details). Plastic bubbles are made in standard sizes, but can be quickly made to order to suit your particular needs. Make sure you get one that is fireproof.

The biggest drawback to having a bubble cover for a recreational area, whether it is a pool, court, or garden party, is that the plastic bubbles are ugly. Many residential areas prohibit their use because of their industrial appearance.

Hopscotch

One of the oldest children's games in the world is hopscotch, and adults never quite outgrow it whether it is chalked on the sidewalk or set indoors in tile or carpet. There are a number of game plans, but the traditional one has ten steps requiring an area of about 5 by 12 feet. This can be modified to be used indoors and set in tile.

Outdoors it can be painted on concrete or whitewashed on the lawn. Most paints deteriorate black-top or asphalt driveways, but the hopscotch design can be set in the asphalt when it is poured by mixing marble or stone dust into the final surfacing to get lighter sections that will contrast with other areas.

Shuffleboard

On the other end of the scale there is shuffleboard. People too old or not inclined to hop around can use long-handled cues to shove wooden disks instead. A shuffleboard court requires a smooth surface of either wood or finely finished concrete. The standard-size shuffleboard field (6 feet by 45 feet) is usually too large to be painted on concrete or stained on wood indoors.

Croquet

Another ancient game, croquet, is sometimes associated with equally ancient Victorian

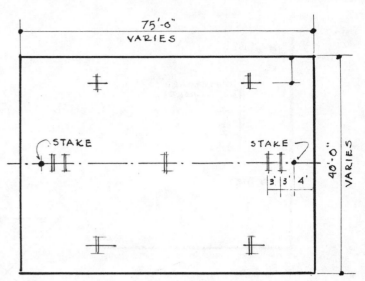

Court layout for croquet, a gentle pastime for long summer evenings.

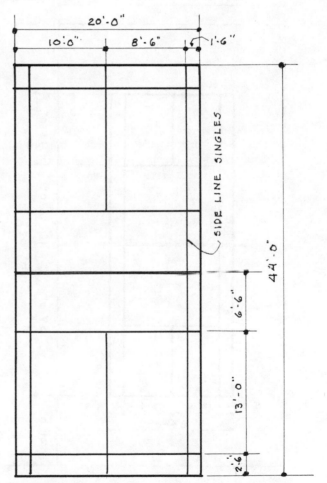

A standard badminton court. Provide extra space on back and sides for movement equal to that of a tennis court.

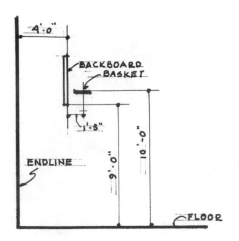
Basketball goal line.

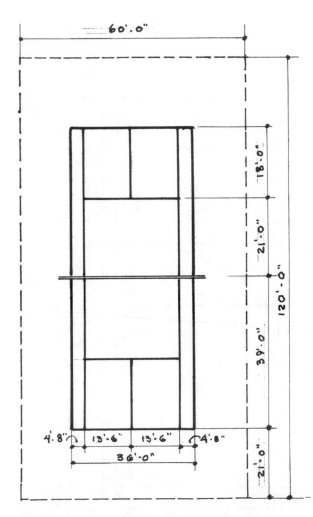
Regulation tennis court. Dotted line indicates fence or enclosure.

ladies in large hats held down with yards of chiffon. But croquet is not necessarily sedate. Players knock wooden balls through wickets, and the playing can become quite heated. The size of the field varies with conditions, but it requires a flat level lawn, 20 to 40 feet wide and 40 to 80 feet long. A few trees will not bother players, and can actually make the game more interesting while providing shade on hot summer days.

Badminton

Like croquet, badminton can be played on a level lawn. It is named after the Duke of Beaufort's, country estate, where it gained popularity because the Duchess was too frail for tennis.

Badminton is most comfortably played on grass, but it can also be played on concrete or a driveway. A standard court is 20 feet wide and 44 feet long, with additional space behind the foul lines for serving. Fences are not required, but windbreaks of trees or hedges should be planted to keep gusts of wind from disrupting games, even when the specially weighted outdoor shuttlecocks are being used.

Basketball

A regular basketball court is a highly finished and polished hardwood floor, 84 by 50 feet for high school basketball and 94 by 50 feet for college basketball. It is highly unlikely that a private citizen can afford this amount and type of playing space, but a form of basketball can usually be played in the driveway. Conventionally, a basket is mounted over the garage door. The basket is 1 foot 6 inches in diameter, and in the driveway or basketball court, it is hung 10 feet high and 4 feet in front of the endline.

Tennis Courts

Tennis courts are expensive pieces of construction. Considerable space is required for a standard court, which is 60 feet wide and 120 feet long. The playing court itself is only 36 feet wide and 78 feet long. The additional space is needed for serving and swinging at balls that bounce over the foul line.

The surface of the tennis court must be absolutely level and pitched to the side with a slope of ½ inch for every 10 feet so water will drain off evenly. If the court is a grass one, subsoil drain tiles are used every 10 feet and no pitch is needed.

The court can be either grass, clay, concrete, composition, or one of a number of playing surfaces that are marketed under brand names. No tennis court is a do-it-yourself project, although the average person can maintain a court with very little or no experience.

Grass is the most elegant surface to play on, although it produces a slightly slower game. It is also a cooler playing surface and produces no glare. Grass must be constantly maintained, and the net and court lines should be changed periodically so the serving and most active playing areas are shifted and the grass can recuperate from the pounding it gets.

Clay is the second-best tennis court surface — in some cases, it is preferred over grass. It produces a faster game than grass, does not reflect as much heat as a harder surface, and has no glare. There is a longer waiting time before you can resume playing after rain than with a grass court, and the surface must be rolled and relined after a heavy storm. Clay must also be dampened and rolled every day of play.

Concrete requires no maintenance and it produces a very fast, if sometimes erratic, game because of the surface flaws. Concrete also retains and reflects heat, especially in the late afternoon. Glare from the sun can be particularly upsetting. Because concrete is so hard and difficult to lay without small pockets and uneven sections, it is not a popular surface for a serious tennis player.

Asphalt is never used for a tennis court surface because it is difficult to make and maintain an acceptable playing surface of asphalt. It is very warm, attracts and reflects heat, and can melt and become sticky in hot summer weather.

There are a number of tennis-court surfaces that are a combination of several different substances. These produce a relatively soft clay-

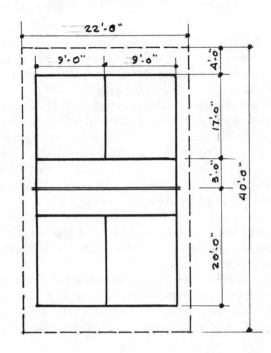

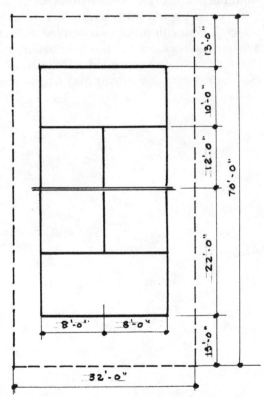

Regulation deck tennis court. Regulation paddle tennis court.

type surface that is easier to maintain and dries faster than clay after a rain. These surfaces are marketed under many different brand names, and are usually green.

In addition to the playing surface, you will have to have net supports and a full or partial enclosure behind the backcourts or you will spend more time chasing balls than playing tennis. A full enclosure is much better than a half or partial enclosure, especially if you are not an expert player.

The enclosure should be a minimum of 10 feet high, at least behind the backcourts. The metal line posts are set in concrete footings, 1 foot square and 3 feet deep.

A distance of 21 feet between the backcourt foul line and enclosure is recommended and considered minimum. On each side, a distance of 12 feet is considered necessary for proper playing.

The preferred orientation for tennis courts is north-northeast, and south-southwest. A player facing the low sun in the late afternoon would be at a serious disadvantage.

To keep up on your tennis game between matches, you can practice on any smooth, windowless wall with a net line painted on it. The court surface can be marked off to indicate half of a tennis court. You can also use a rebound net, stretched on a metal frame for practicing serves and returns. The net gives a slower return than a solid wall, closer to the return from another player. There is a few seconds' delay as the ball is caught and stretches the nylon net, which then hurls it back at the reverse angle at which it was hit into the net.

Paddle Tennis

A game similar to regular tennis, paddle tennis is played with a 9-inch-wide and 16½-inch-long paddle. The ball used is a deadened tennis ball, and the major difference is in the size of the court required.

Paddle tennis is played on a much smaller court than racket tennis, one 20 feet wide and 44 feet long for official play. You must allow 13 feet between the backcourt foul line and the enclosure, and 6 feet on each side. The entire space needed for a paddle tennis court is 32 feet wide and 70 feet long.

Although paddle tennis is a fast game, the deadened ball does not have the bounce of a regular tennis ball. Consequently, a lower enclosure is permissible for paddle tennis. Usually a full or partial enclosure only 8 feet high is sufficient for the average player.

Glossary

Anchor bolt A heavy bolt imbedded in masonry to secure a wooden sill to the foundation.

Angle iron An L-shaped strip of metal used to support masonry over openings.

Apron A finished piece of wood below the sill of a window used to cover the rough edge.

Ash dump A metal frame with a metal door placed in the floor of a fireplace through which ashes are disposed of by being dumped into the ash pit at the base of the chimney.

Asphalt A mineral pitch or tar used on built-up roofs and the exterior foundation walls of basements to waterproof them.

Awning window A pane of glass or a series of panes set in a frame and opening outward from the bottom.

Back bar An arrangement of cabinets, shelves and counterspace behind the bar itself for the display and storage of glassware and bottles.

Back filling Soil and broken stones used to level around the foundation walls and provide a slope for water to be drained away from the house.

Balustrade A railing made up of posts connected at the top by a handrail.

Base shoe A strip of molding nailed to the baseboard next to the floor.

Battens Thin narrow strips of wood used to cover joints in vertical wood siding.

Batts Insulating material composed of mineral fiber with a vapor barrier on one side, sized to fit between stud walls, joists, and rafters.

Beam A large piece of timber or metal used to support floor and ceiling joists.

Bearing plate A metal plate placed under a column or beam to distribute the weight of the load.

Bearing wall A wall that carries the load from floor joists and partitions above it.

Blistering A defect in which paint film pulls away from the surface painted.

Board foot A unit of measure for lumber. One board foot would be a piece of lumber 1 foot square and approximately 1 inch thick.

Bond The pattern in which brickwork is done.

Bow window Glass panes set in a frame on a continuous curve.

Box out A term meaning to cover columns, beams, pipes, or wiring with another material to improve their appearance.

Branch pipe A special plumbing pipe with one or more branches.

Brick veneer A layer of brick, one brick thick, attached to the surface of a wall, but carrying no load except its own weight.

Bridging Pieces of wood or metal straps crisscrossed between joists to stiffen them and hold them in place.

Building line The limit to which you are permitted to build or extend your house in relation to the edge of your property.

Built-up beam A beam formed by nailing or bolting two or more planks together to increase their strength.

Cantilever A structural overhang projecting beyond the supporting wall or column.

Carpenter's square A steel framing-square, usually measuring 25 by 16 inches, used for measurements and to lay out right angles.

Cased opening A finished opening with trim, but no door.

Casement A window hinged on its vertical edge.

Casing Framework around a window or door.

Chalking The powdering of the top surface of paint.

Cinder block Building block made of cement and cinders. Used because it is light in weight.

Clapboard Long boards, thin on top and thicker on bottom, used horizontally for siding.

Clerestory A wall containing windows raised above surrounding roofs.

Collar beam A horizontal tie beam connecting, and parallel to, two opposite rafters.

Condensation Warm, moist air changing to drops of water on a cold surface, such as glass or metal.

Coping   The top course of a masonry wall.

Corner boards   Vertical boards used to trim the corner of an exterior frame wall.

Cornice   The decorative construction at the intersection of the roof and side wall at the eaves.

Course   A level row of brick or masonry in a wall.

Crawl space   The unexcavated space enclosed by the foundation walls under the first floor of a house.

Creosote   An oily liquid, made primarily from coal tar, which serves as a wood preservative.

Cupola   A small domed structure on a roof to allow for interior lighting or serve as a lookout. It may be also simply decorative.

Dead load   Weight of structure and finishing materials carried by joist and structural walls and beams.

Delaminate   A separation of plywood plys due to moisture.

Dormer   A roofed structure, cut into a sloping roof, containing a vertical window.

Double-hung window   A window with upper and lower vertical sliding sashes.

Down light   An incandescent light fixture recessed into the ceiling so that only the floor or furniture under the fixture is lighted.

Dress   To smooth and finish wood or masonry.

Dressed-size lumber   A term referring to the actual size of lumber. For instance, a 2-by-4 stud is really 1⅝ inches by 3⅝ inches.

Dry stone wall   A masonry wall laid without mortar.

Dry wall   This term refers to any interior wall finish that does not use plaster. However, it usually means ⅜-inch or ½-inch gypsum wallboard or Sheetrock with the joints taped and spackled.

Dry well   An excavation in porous soil loosely filled with rocks, rubble, or gravel. The well receives water from drains and allows it to seep away.

Ducts   Large rectangular or round tubes used to distribute air from the furnace or air-conditioning unit to registers in the rooms. They may be constructed of plastic, metal, asbestos, or composition materials.

Dutch door   A door divided horizontally so the top half may be opened while the lower section remains closed.

Easement   An acquired right to use part of the land belonging to someone else.

Eaves   The part of the roof that projects over the side walls.

Efflorescence   White powder that forms on the surface of brick and masonry.

Eyebrow dormer   A low window in a roof over which the roof is carried in a wavy line similar to an arch.

Facade   The exterior appearance of a house or elevation.

Fascia   The flat horizontal board at the outer face of the cornice.

Fenestration   The arrangement and design of doors and windows in a wall.

Finish floor   Hardwood, tile, or carpet laid over the subfloor.

Finish hardware   Doorknobs, locks, hinges, and any exposed hardware in a house.

Fire stops   The blocking of air passages to prevent the spread of fire within the wall.

Flashing   Sheet metal used at all intersections of walls and roofs, at changes in materials, and over doors and windows to prevent the leakage of water into the house.

Floating   Bringing a smooth finish to cement or concrete.

Footing   The foundation for a column or a wall which distributes the weight carried by the column or wall over a greater area. Footings are usually concrete and are placed below the frost line to prevent structural damage from freezing.

Forms   Enclosures made with wood or metal to shape and hold the wet ("green") concrete until it has set and dried sufficiently to support itself and imposed loads.

Frame construction   The type of building which is made of lumber using wood studs, joists, and beams.

Framing   The process of putting together the studs, joists, beams, plates, flooring, roofing, and partitions to build a house.

Franklin stove   An iron fireplace, named after Benjamin Franklin, which made its appearance in Philadelphia in great numbers between 1785 and 1830.

Furring The act of applying furring strips to provide an air space between structural walls and the interior finish or to level an uneven surface.

Furring strips Narrow strips of wood or metal.

Gable The triangular portion of an end wall contained between the sloping eaves of a ridge roof.

Gambrel roof A ridge roof with a double slope, the lower slope being the steeper of the two.

Garret window A skylight with the glass incorporated into the slope of the roof.

Gazebo A summer house in a garden.

Glaze The installation of glass in windows and doors.

Glazed tile Masonry tile with a hard glossy surface.

Grade A term for ground level. Also, to fill earth in around a building so water will drain away from the foundation, and to smooth and properly level a driveway.

Grasscloth A highly textured wallpaper made from woven threads and grass.

Grout A cement mixture used to fill crevices.

Half-story The attic in a pitched roof with sloping walls, having some flat ceiling and a floor.

Hardpan A compacted layer of earth and clay which is very difficult to excavate.

Hardwood It does not refer to the actual hardness of the wood, but to a botanical group of trees, such as maple, oak, and other broad-leafed trees.

Hip roof A ridge roof in which the gables have been replaced by sloping sections of roof.

Hollow-core doors Interior doors, often used for closets, consisting of two thin sheets of plywood glued to a frame.

Hopper window A window sash with hinges at the bottom and opening into the room.

Hung ceiling A lightweight ceiling made up of panels suspended in a grid system and held by inverted-T runners.

Hydrostatic head Water pressure from a high-water table on the underside of the basement floors and walls that forces moisture and water into the basement.

I-beam A steel beam in the shape of a capital I; used many times in remodeling to support walls and floors when the structural partitions and bearing walls have been removed.

Indirect lighting A system of lighting the walls and ceiling of a room with fixtures that cannot be seen.

Inglenook A Scandinavian word meaning built-in seating close to and around the fireplace.

Jalousie window Unframed strips of glass set in a series that opens from the bottom to prevent rain from coming into the house.

Jamb The vertical side posts used in framing a door or window.

Joist One of a number of timbers used to support floors and ceilings. Joists are used in series set edgewise, and are in turn supported by bearing walls, structural partitions, or beams.

Kiln-dried A term used to refer to lumber that has been dried in a kiln with controlled heat and humidity to artificially season it.

Knee wall A low wall in the attic running parallel to the ridge that closes off the unusable triangular section next to the floor.

Lally column A round steel pipe, usually 4 inches in diameter and sometimes filled with concrete, used to support beams.

Lath Small strips of wood about ⅜ inch thick and 1 inch wide, used to support plaster, seal cracks between boards, and build decorative screens. Wood lath for use with plaster has been replaced by metal lath in the few areas in which plaster is still used.

Leader A pipe or down spout that carries rainwater from the gutter to the ground.

Lean-to A small addition having a shed roof which is supported by the wall of the house.

Lien A legal claim against the owner of a house by a contractor who has not been paid for work and materials supplied.

Light A single windowpane.

Light well A walled and drained excavation outside a below-ground window that allows for natural lighting and ventilation.

Line level A lightweight instrument containing a bubble tube that is suspended from taut string to check the level of two widely separated points.

Lineal foot A line 1 foot long, as distinguished from a square foot or a cubic foot.

Lintel A steel, wood, or stone beam placed horizontally over an opening in a wall to support the wall above it.

Live load Weight of furniture and occupants on joist and structural walls and beams.

Loft A room or platform directly under the roof.

Loggia An arcade with a roof and one open side.

Lot line The outer perimeters of your property, not to be confused with the building line determined by the set-back regulations in the zoning ordinance.

Louver An opening for ventilation containing slanted members to keep out rain.

Mansard roof A type of roof having two slopes, the lower one very steep and almost vertical, the upper one almost flat.

Mastic A thick adhesive used for bedding glass, setting tile, and repairing roofs.

Modular design and construction Using a module of 4 feet so residential work is more economical and there is less waste. Studs and joists are placed on 16-inch centers with a ceiling height of 8 feet, which permits plywood and interior finishes to be used without cutting and waste since they are manufactured in sheets 4 feet by 8 feet.

Module A unit of measure used by architects and designers.

Mortar A malleable-when-wet building material, usually a cement or plaster mixture, used for masonry or walls.

Mullion The vertical division between a series of windows. Generally included in the term "muntin."

Muntin The division between windowpanes both vertical and horizontal.

Nailing strips Pieces of wood to which finish material is nailed; similar to furring strips.

Nosing The rounded edge of a stair tread.

Orientation The location of the house—the direction it faces.

Overhang The projection of a floor or roof over an outside wall.

Overloading Placing too much weight on a beam, column, or a floor.

Parquet floor Pieces of wood set in a pattern.

Partition An interior dividing wall which carries no load, only its own weight.

Party wall A structural wall shared by two houses.

Pavilion A structure or canopied area in a garden or recreation area which is used for entertainment or shelter.

Penny A term denoting nail length, originally derived from the cost per hundred. Lengths vary slightly, but in general a 2d (the "d" stands for penny) nail is 1 inch long, the 4d is 1½ inches, the 6d is 2 inches, the 8d is 2½ inches, the 10d is 3 inches, the 20d is 4 inches, and the 60d is 6 inches.

Perspective drawing A sketch of a house taken from a particular location.

Pilaster A column attached to a wall.

Pillar A supporting masonry shaft made of smaller pieces of marble, stone, or brick. It differs from a column in that a column is one solid piece.

Pin spots Incandescent lights recessed into the ceiling for special lighting effects, such as lighting a sculpture or flower arrangement.

Pitch Various combinations of coal tar insoluble in water and used in plumbing and other construction work, or, the angle of slope on a roof.

Plank A heavy piece of timber thicker than a board, usually 1½ inches thick and more than 6 inches wide.

Plasterboard Gypsum that is covered on both sides with paper, often called dry wall or gypboard.

Plate A 2-by-4 or larger piece of lumber placed on top of a stud wall or masonry so that joists and rafters may be fastened to it.

Plumb bob A weight attached to a string (plumb line) for testing the trueness of perpendicular surfaces.

Pointing Finishing of joints in a masonry wall.

Portico An open space attached to a house as a porch, or completely detached with a roof supported with columns.

Porte cochere A covered automobile entrance connecting the driveway to the front door.

Portland cement Silica, lime, and alumnia mixed together and fired in a kiln. The clinkers are then ground fine to produce a strong hydraulic cement.

Priming The first coat of paint, usually a special primer, put on wood or metal to make a hard opaque surface that will take additional coats of paint well.

Quarry-faced masonry A rough squared stone with the face as it was split in the quarry.

Quarry-tile Machine-made unglazed tile of a reddish-brown color.

Quarter round A molding that is a quarter of a circle.

Rabbet A section cut out of wood and timber to receive another board cut to fit it.

Radiant heating A system of heating that uses the floor, walls, or ceiling as a heating panel, with warmed pipes or wires imbedded in it.

Rafter The sloping member of the roof structure that runs from the plate to the ridge.

Reinforced concrete Concrete that has been given greater strength by steel bars imbedded in it.

Retaining wall A wall built to hold back the soil.

Return The continuation of a molding in another direction.

Rheostat An electrical device regulating current to light fixtures so the brightness can be controlled.

Ridge The top of the roof where two slopes meet.

Riser The vertical board under the tread of a step.

Rock wool A product manufactured from granite, silica, calcium, and magnesium that looks like wool, but is vermin-, fire-, and damp-proof and is used as insulation.

Rough floor A subfloor that serves as a base for the finished flooring material.

Rough opening An unfinished opening in which the window and door frames will be placed.

Saddle The ridge covering of a roof. Also a board or marble covering the floor joint in a doorway where the material changes from wood to tile.

Sash The frame for one or more windowpanes.

Scale Architects do drawings to scale, denoting the size of the drawings in relation to the full size house: i.e., ¼ inch = 1 foot means that ¼ inch on the drawings represents 1 foot in the actual house. The architect does this measuring and drawing with an expensive ruler, also called a scale. Architects also speak of scale in relation to appropriateness and proportion of elements in the design of a house. If something is out of scale, it is either too large or too small for the rest of the house (or room).

Sheathing Plywood or boards nailed to the studs and roof rafters on the exterior of a house as a foundation for the finish siding and roofing.

Shed roof A roof sloping in one direction with a single pitch.

Shim A thin, tapered piece of shingle used in leveling work.

Shingle Thin pieces of tapered wood or other material used to cover walls or roofs.

Shore A piece of timber used as a temporary support.

Side lights Small vertical windows on each side of a door.

Sill The lowest horizontal member of a frame supporting a house, or the lowest member under a door or a window.

Skylight An opening in a roof that is covered with a transparent or translucent material in order to admit light.

Sleepers Strips of wood laid over rough concrete floors so a finished wood floor can be applied over them.

Soffit The underside of overhangs.

Soil pipe A vertical pipe carrying off waste from the toilet.

Sole plate The horizontal member placed at the floor line of a partition.

Spackle To apply a paste of Spackle powder and water to fill cracks in a surface prior to painting.

Span The distance between supports for joist and rafters.

Square A term denoting roofing materials measuring 100 square feet.

Stick built Not prefabricated in any way. Built stud by stud and joist by joist.

Stud A vertical piece of lumber, usually a 2-by-4, used in concert with others to form walls and partitions.

Subfloor The plywood or boards applied directly to the floor joists as part of the rough work. The finished floor is placed on top of the subfloor.

Template A gauge or pattern to be followed in doing work. Also, a stone block or short timber placed horizontally under a beam to distribute the weight, as over a doorway.

Terrazzo A mixture of marble chips and cement, ground and polished smooth. It is used for floors and can be given a high polish.

Thermostat An electrically controlled device to regulate the heat and air conditioning.

Three-way switch An electric switch that allows a light fixture to be controlled from two separate places.

Tie beam A beam that prevents the spreading apart of rafters.

Toenailing Nailing at an angle to attach one piece of lumber to another.

Top plate The horizontal member nailed to the top of a partition.

Transite Manufactured fireproof sheets made of a combination of asbestos and cement.

Transom A window over a door or over another window.

Trap A vertical bend in the water pipe of each plumbing fixture that stays full of water and prevents offensive odors from entering the house or a room of a house.

Trowel A flat steel tool used to spread and smooth mortar and cement.

Truss A combination of wood or steel members that work together to span distances that none could approach alone.

Vapor barrier Material used to keep moisture from penetrating walls.

Variance Written permission from a zoning board to build or remodel in a specific acceptable manner.

Veneered wall Brick or stone that is not bonded together, but attached to a frame wall with clips, and does not carry any load but its own weight.

Wainscot A lining or paneling for the lower part of an interior wall.

Wallboard Gypsum, wood, plastic, and many other materials that are used to finish walls on the interior of a house and around a shower or tub.

Weatherstrip A flange of metal or plastic covering joints to keep out drafts around doors and windows.

Wet bar A bar that contains a sink and plumbing.

Wet wall A term referring to walls that contain soil pipes, hot- and cold-water pipes, and vents.

Winders Treads of stairs shaped like a triangle and used at corners.

Index*